THE
NASTY
QUOTE
B·O·O·K

Compiled by
COLIN M. JARMAN

Gramercy Books
New York

This 2001 edition is published by Gramercy Books™, an imprint
of Random House Value Publishing, Inc., 280 Park Avenue,
New York, NY 10017, by arrangement with NTC/Contemporary
Books.

Gramercy Books™ and design are trademarks of Random House
Value Publishing, Inc.

Printed in the United States of America

(Originally published as: *Barbed Quotes*)

Random House
New York · Toronto · London · Sydney · Auckland
http://www.randomhouse.com/

Library of Congress Cataloging-in-Publication Data

Barbed quotes.
     The nasty quote book / compiled by Colin M. Jarman.
          p. cm.
     Originally published: Barbed quotes. Lincolnwood, Ill. :
     Contemporary Books, c1999.
     ISBN 0-517-16384-5
          1. Quotations, English. 2. Wit and humor. 3. Invective.
          I. Jarman, Colin, 1958- II.
     Title.

PN6084.H8 B37 2001
082—dc21

                                                    2001023193

9 8 7 6 5 4 3 2 1

CONTENTS

INTRODUCTION

The point of quotations is
that one can use another's words to be insulting.

—Amanda Cross
(Carolyn Heilbrun)

No one can be as calculatedly rude
as the British, which amazes Americans,
who do not understand studied insult and
can only offer abuse as a substitute.

—Paul Gallico

Paul Gallico's observation perfectly sums up my intentions for this celebratory collection of insult and abuse. In *Barbed Quotes*, I have combined the slightly different approaches to name-calling of the Americans and the British. Just as the USA and the UK are "two nations separated by a common language," we are also distinguishable in the way we insult and abuse.

Although most of the targets in this volume are household names across North America, there may be some names among those throwing the mud who will not be quite so familiar. The vast majority of these unknown names will probably be the vitriolic voyeurs and caustic castigators of barbed ire from Great Britain. Whether writing for the respected *Times* of London or appearing on the esteemed BBC-TV, they have a personal prescription of poison noticeably different from that of their more well-known colleagues in the United States.

I hope that as you browse through *Barbed Quotes*, you'll make up your own mind as to which country is ruder. After ten years of collecting insults from around the world, I have yet to come across any nation as rude as us British. Get us talking on politics, sport, food, fashion—any subject—and we become world-beaters in hissing and dissing. Insult in Great Britain has almost been elevated to the level of an Olympic sport.

With that thought in mind, dip into this volume to decide who would win the Battle of the Bile—the United Slates of America or Ingrate Britain?

Colin M. Jarman
London, England (1999)

1
ACTORS AND ACTRESSES

Actors and actresses are so stupid, ignorant, and eaten up with themselves that one can easily forget how lazy they are. Many cannot face the effort of articulating clearly enough to be understood. . . . Anything like that is too much trouble—beside the point, in fact, if all you care about is receiving attention and looking good.

Kingsley Amis
The Spectator *(1988)*

A sign of a celebrity is often that his name is worth more than his services.

Daniel J. Boorstin
The Image *(1962)*

I don't really find any silent comedians funny. . . . I don't really identify with it. I've never had to wallpaper a room while delivering a piano upstairs.

Angus Deayton (1992)

When actors begin to think, it's time for a change. They are not fitted for it.

Stephen Leacock
The Decline of Drama
(1921)

Actors, particularly bad ones, in Restoration costume, look exactly like caterpillars on their hind legs.

C. A. Lejeune (1945)

In show business most of what you do is fakery and who wants to spend their whole life with a bunch of fakes?

Marcel Orphuls (1990)

Acting is largely a matter of farting about in disguises.

Peter O'Toole

Actors in Canada are a little too much of the fly-by-night order to hold a high social status.

Horton Rhys (1861)

I've written for the theater for many years, and I'd never vote for an actor to represent me for anything.

Irwin Shaw

Anonymous
If she was cast as Lady Godiva the horse would steal the show.

Anonymous

The fellow is such a ham I bet he wears a clove in his buttonhole.

Irving "Swifty" Lazar

Danny Aiello (b 1935)
"Dellaventura" (1997)—Fearless Fosdick, the marionette detective derived from an Al Capp character for a short-lived '50s puppet show, was actually less wooden than Aiello is. Lighter on his feet, too, of course. . . . William Conrad was more agile in "Jake and the Fat Man." Even the old-timers in the Suscatal commercial are more sprightly.

Tom Shales
Washington Post

Alan Alda (b 1936)
Betsy's Wedding (1990)—A wacky wedding, courtesy Alan Alda, whose persona is beginning to grate.

Virgin Film Guide

Kirstie Alley (b 1955)
"Veronica's Closet" (1997)—It has Kirstie Alley, large
and unwieldy and tottery.

> Tom Shales
> Washington Post

Gillian Anderson (b 1968)
"The X-Files" (1997)—Anderson is fairly credible as
Scully, and some of us think she's cute as a button, but
"cute" ain't the same as "good actin'," and sadly,
Gillian's open-mouthed, bug-eyed look is getting a bit
tired.

> The Vidiots

Loni Anderson (b 1945)
"Melrose Place" (1996)—As a beauty consultant's
overly coiffed mum . . . she couldn't have looked less
natural if she were wearing one of Burt Reynolds's old
rugs.

> Entertainment Weekly

Pamela Anderson (Lee) (b 1967)
Without "Baywatch," her breasts will last longer than
her career.

> Peter Ko (1997)

On Anderson's marriage to Tommy Lee—Their love was
like their tattoos: painful, cheap, and skin-deep.

> Jim Mullen
> Entertainment Weekly (1996)

A former classmate of Pamela's said that in high school, she was flat-chested. That's shocking—I had no idea she had graduated high school.

> *Conan O'Brien*
> *"Late Night" (1996)*

Because of her lavish spending habits, Pamela is said to be having financial troubles. Which is strange, because her two largest assets are liquid.

> *Conan O'Brien*
> *"Late Night" (1996)*

Barb Wire (1996)—The artificially endowed Pamela Anderson Lee portrays the titular heroine. . . . Her acting is less colorful than her wardrobe.

> *Robert Seulowitz*
> Monthly Film Bulletin

Julie Andrews (b 1934)
There's a kind of flowering dullness about her, a boredom in rowdy bloom.

> *Joyce Haber*

Anne Archer (b 1947)
Patriot Games (1992)—Her insufferably goody-goody performance makes you wish Glenn Close would show up brandishing a kitchen knife.

> Virgin Film Guide

Tom Arnold (b 1959)
The Stupids (1996)—Starring Tom Arnold. A
documentary, no doubt.

> *Jim Mullen*
> Entertainment Weekly

"The Tom Show" (1997)—Yet another futile attempt
to make a TV star out of hapless comic Tom Arnold.

> *Tom Shales*
> Washington Post

Rowan Atkinson (b 1955)
When hopeful journalism students in creative writing
courses ask me for a definition of an oxymoron I
always say Rowan Atkinson as "Personality of the
Year."

> *A. A. Gill*
> The Times *of London (1995)*

"One-man Show" (1990)—It's not inconceivable that
this comic's biggest fans at home are products of an
upbringing that encourages boys to tame their nasty
bowel habits at an early age, with the consequence that
their obsession with alimentary products persists right
through to Oxford and Cambridge.

> *Frank Rich*
> New York Times

Dan Aykroyd (b 1952)

Sneakers (1992)—Dan needs a few more workouts, although he's been having trouble in the weight department for a good few movies now.

> *Patrick Boyle*
> Modern Review

"Soul Man" (1997)—It's a sorry sight to see the once wild-and-crazy guy selling his soul for sitcom success.

> *Bruce Fretts*
> Entertainment Weekly

Lauren Bacall (b 1924)

On Bacall's seventieth birthday—Her hair lounges on her shoulders like an anesthetized cocker spaniel.

> *Henry Allen*
> Washington Post *(1994)*

Applause (1973)—It doesn't actually matter that she is not notably expert at singing or dancing. . . . What does matter about Miss Bacall is that she's no great shakes at acting either, so there is a curious vacuum where the middle of the show ought to be.

> *Sheridan Morley*

Scott Baio (b 1961)
Scott Baio has a track record of late ("Diagnosis Murder," "Charles in Charge," "Baby Talk") that leaves most people busing tables.

Peter Ko (1997)

Alec Baldwin (b 1958)
Caribbean blue eyes. The knowing mouth. A fine figure that stops just this side of martial artistry. These are the anonymous good looks of an afternoon actor.

Richard Corliss
Time *(1990)*

Curdled (1996)—Baldwin's psycho killer is about as terrifying as a flapjack.

Mike D'Angelo
Entertainment Weekly

Lucille Ball (1910–89)
"The Lucy Show" (1986)—It is not funny watching a seventy-something-year-old woman act like she's still forty, trying to get a laugh with slapstick antics. . . . It's like rubbing the audience's nose in the fact that we're all a lot older and not particularly better.

John Javna
The Best of TV Sitcoms
(1988)

Mame (1974)—So terrible it isn't boring; you can get fixated staring at it and wondering what Lucille Ball thought she was doing.

New Yorker *(1977)*

Anne Bancroft (b 1931)
The Little Foxes (1967)—Her acting suggests a high school girl with undue hopes of becoming the star of her college dramatic club.

John Simon

Diana Barrymore (1921–60)
Diana is a horse's arse, quite a pretty one, but still a horse's arse.

John Barrymore

John Barrymore (1882–1942)
Conspicuously unclean and smelled highly on occasions.

David Niven

Kim Basinger (b 1953)
Cool World (1992)—Casting Kim as a two-dimensional doxy—one could almost say a "little tramp"—was a stroke of genius.

Anne Billson

Cool World (1992)—After a career of steam-heated movies Kim Basinger ends up as only a sexy cartoon. . . . But the cartoon acts better than she does.

Tom Hutchinson

I love my job, and, with the exception of Kim Basinger, most of the people I work with.

Jeffrey Katzenberg
Variety

Stephanie Beacham (b 1947)

The Rover (1987)—Stephanie Beacham comes on dressed like an especially exotic wedding cake to do an eccentric impersonation of a period Zsa Zsa Gabor.

Sheridan Morley

Warren Beatty (b 1937)

The only reason he had a child is so that he can meet babysitters.

David Letterman
"The Late Show" (1991)

Heaven Can Wait (1978)—The more Beatty concentrates, the more glazed and distracted he looks.

Virgin Film Guide

James Belushi (b 1954)

Traces of Red (1992)—The decidedly tubby Belushi hardly qualifying as the epitome of a smoldering sex god.

> Kim Newman
> Empire *magazine*

Dirk Benedict (b 1945)

Blue Tornado (1991)—Benedict has at least had a decent haircut since "Battlestar Galactica"—but still acts like a square-jawed sequoia.

> Empire *magazine*

Jack Benny (1894–1974)

When he has a party, you not only bring your own scotch, you bring your own rocks.

> George Burns

Barbi Benton (b 1950)

Sugar Time!—One of my rules was: If they are desperate enough to use Barbi Benton in it, it can't be any good. There was no need to review it. Just say, "Barbi Benton was in it."

> Peter Farrell
> Oregonian

Ingrid Bergman (1915–82)

Turning down the role of Rick in Casablanca—I don't want to star opposite an unknown Swedish broad.

> George Raft

Milton Berle (b 1908)
He's done everybody's act. He's a parrot with skin on.

Fred Allen

Sandra Bernhard (b 1955)
She is as much fun as barbed wire.

Tom Hutchinson

Ted Bessell (1935–96)
"Me and the Chimp"—It's a testimony to Ted Bessell
that he wasn't outacted too badly by the chimpanzee.

Jeff Bordern
Charlotte Observer

Richard Beymer (b 1938)
West Side Story (1961)—Beymer seems like something
scraped out of a pie.

Ethan Mordden
The Hollywood Musical
(1981)

Sissy Bigger
"Ready, Set, Cook" (1997)—What's not so much fun
is the intrusive voice of Sissy Bigger, who comes across
as a disconcerting pest.

William Rice
Chicago Tribune

Humphrey Bogart (1899–1957)

After directing Bogart in Sabrina—I look at you, Bogey, and beneath the surface of an apparent shit, I see the face of a real shit.

Billy Wilder

Brian Bosworth (b 1965)

Stone Cold (1991)—Bosworth has hair like a blow-dried skunk and a neck twice the size of his head. The Boz has all the superstar charisma of the average forklift truck and could take acting lessons from Flipper.

Empire *magazine*

Lorraine Bracco (b 1955)

Medicine Man (1992)—Ms. Bracco squeaks like a sugar bat.

Maureen Paton

Kenneth Branagh (b 1960)

If you smeared Germolene over those lips, his mouth would heal over.

Anonymous

Henry V (1989)—The film's visual tedium, vulgarity, and musical mediocrity would be more bearable if Branagh himself were a more persuasive lead actor.

Monthly Film Bulletin

Marlon Brando (b 1924)
Brando, his heart it bleeds for the masses,
But the people he works with, he kicks in the asses.

Anonymous

An angel as a man, a monster as an actor.

Bernardo Bertolucci

The Godfather, Part II (1972)—What made Part II
slightly more attractive is the absence of Marlon
Brando's unpardonably cheap performance.

John Simon (1974)

The most overrated actor in the world.

Frank Sinatra

Columbus: The Discovery (1992)—He was paid
3 million pounds for his last role—Torquemada—and
by the look of him he blew it all on lunch.

The Times *of London (1994)*

Sarah Brightman

Phantom of the Opera (1989)—She reveals little competence as an actress. After months of playing *Phantom* in London, she still simulates fear and affection alike by screwing her face into bug-eyed, chipmunk-cheeked poses more appropriate to the Lon Chaney film version.

> *Frank Rich*
> New York Times

Pierce Brosnan (b 1952)

GoldenEye (1995)—The man looks as though he was born to model jumpers.

> *Tom Shone*
> The Times *of London*

Blair Brown (b 1948)

The Secret Rapture (1989)—A matter of lofty smiles and holier-than-thou posturings.

> *Frank Rich*
> New York Times

James Brown

"World's Funniest . . ." TV series—James "I'll Do Anything to Keep My Cushy Job" Brown hosts. America weeps.

> *Peter Ko (1997)*

Yul Brynner (1915–1985)

He was one of the biggest shits I've ever come across in show business.

Jeffrey Bernard

Westworld (1973)—Brynner is extremely well cast as a robot, especially if you saw him in *Adios, Sabata.*

Monthly Film Bulletin

Richard Burton (1925–84)

The rudest man I've ever met, and unattractive— pockmarked as an Easter Island statue.

Libby Purves

James Cagney (1899–1986)

He's just a little runt.

Howard Hughes (1927)

Michael Caine (b 1933)

When you watch Caine act, even in his best stuff . . . do you ever think: "Hey, I bet there's a really fascinating man under there with hundreds of secrets"? Of course not. You think: "Holy shit, this guy is dull as Labradors."

Simon Garfield

In truth, he is an overfat, flatulent, 62-year-old windbag, a master of inconsequence now masquerading as a guru, passing off his vast limitations as pious virtues.

Richard Harris (1995)

A mediocrity with halitosis.

Peter Langan

Michael Caine (b 1933) **and Roger Moore** (b 1927)
Bullseye! (1990)—Few leading actors as feeble, lazy, and self-indulgent as Caine and Moore are in this film could reasonably expect to work again.

Christopher Tookey

Capucine (1933-90)
During filming of Walk on the Wild Side—If you were more of a woman, I would be more of a man. Kissing you is like kissing the side of a beer bottle.

Laurence Harvey (1962)

David Caruso
On Caruso's returning to TV after quitting "NYPD Blue" for Hollywood—Limping back after a couple of movies that did at the box office what a Yugo would do at Le Mans.

Steve Johnson
Chicago Tribune

On Caruso's return to TV—What was meant to be a shrewd career maneuver turned out on a par with Napoleon's decision to invade Russia.

Tom Shales
Washington Post *(1997)*

Charlie Chaplin (1889–1977)
The son of a bitch is a ballet dancer . . . and if I get a chance, I'll kill him with my bare hands.

W. C. Fields

I have no doubt that Albert Einstein's name will still be remembered and revered when Lloyd George, Marshall Foch, and William Hohenzollern share with Charlie Chaplin that ineluctable oblivion which awaits the uncreative mind.

J. B. S. Haldane
Daedalus

The Great Dictator (1940)—He is not a good preacher. Indeed, he is frighteningly bad.

John O'Hara

Chaplin was a most terrible phony.

Laurence Olivier (1979)

Cher (b 1946)

She's got a commercial. She goes, "I call my perfume uninhibited, 'cause there are so many different people in me." Yeah, and they're all under eighteen.

Joy Behar (1993)

Andrew "Dice" Clay (b 1957)

The Freddy Krueger of scumbag comedians. . . . Put the stake of public indifference through his shriveled heart, one-two-three times. He still comes back for more.

Steve Johnson
Chicago Tribune *(1997)*

If you said irony to Clay, he'd look down at his shirt and think it needed pressing.

Denis Leary

Claudette Colbert (1903–96)

I'd wring your neck . . . if you had one.

Noël Coward

An ugly shopgirl.

Marlene Dietrich

Joan Collins (b 1933)

"Pacific Palisades" (1997)—This show needs more sex, not sexagenarians.

Bruce Fretts
Entertainment Weekly

At the 1989 Cannes Film Festival—She looked like a bag lady.

Lenny Henry

I said she was known on the show as the "British Open."

Joan Rivers

Nancy Reagan has had a facelift. Joan Collins, on the other hand, uses a forklift.

Joan Rivers

Cristi Conaway
"Timecop" (1997)—Every traveling salesman's idea of a hot number.

Steve Johnson
Chicago Tribune

Sean Connery (b 1929)
From Russia with Love (1963)—The sadistic, suave agent is again played by Connery and although he is not very good at it, it seems to be where he belongs.

Stanley Kauffmann
The New Republic

David Copperfield (b 1956)
The aesthetically challenged magician . . . shame he can't do a trick with his face.

London Evening Standard
(1994)

Kevin Costner (b 1955)

Dances with Wolves (1990)—Costner has feathers in his hair and feathers in his head.

Pauline Kael

Costner is a two- rather than a three-note actor, capable but unimaginative, and when he has to pull the plug out at the end, there's not much water left in the bath.

Derek Malcolm (1993)

The Bodyguard (1992)—Sporting the type of Haircut from Hell Harrison Ford had in *Presumed Innocent*, and swigging orange juice in an attempt at depth.

Mark Salisbury
Empire *magazine*

A Perfect World (1993)—In a perfect world . . . there would be an injunction against Kevin Costner doing death scenes, especially as long and meandering as a cross-Texas road trip.

Virgin Film Guide

Tom Courtenay (b 1937)

Charley's Aunt (1971)—Tom Courtenay, as Charley's aunt, reminded me of Whistler's mother.

Frank Marcus

Joan Crawford (1906-77)

Joan always cries a lot. Her tear ducts must be close to her bladder.

Bette Davis

Macaulay Culkin (b 1980)

Home Alone 2 (1992)—He is performing less like a natural-born son of celluloid and more like a hardened professional. You can almost see him calculating his fee as he delivers his smug one-liners and nauseating dollops of folksy wisdom.

Anne Billson

Grow up—fast! Then we can forget you.

Alexander Walker
London Evening Standard
(1993)

Tim Curry (b 1946)

"Over the Top" (1996)—Was there ever a more apt name for a project starring Tim Curry?

Ben Boychuk

Tyne Daly (b 1947)

Tyne Daly won an Emmy this year for best supporting actress in a drama. If you can name the show, you need to seriously re-examine your life's priorities.

Peter Ko (1997)

Tony Danza (b 1950)

"The Tony Danza Show" (1997)—The Energizer bunny of situation comedy. . . . No sitcom star is more eager to be liked, and it becomes suffocating to watch. If we all send him a biscuit and a pat on the head, maybe he'll go sit in a corner somewhere.

> *Steve Johnson*
> Chicago Tribune

Lolita Davidovich (b 1961)

Intersection (1994)—Lolita, a kind of cross between Julia Roberts and Jack Nicholson.

> *Jeremy Novick*
> Modern Review

John Davidson (b 1941)

On Davidson's having costarred with future Oscar winner Sally Field in The Girl with Something Extra—John Davidson developed into a piece of plastic and went on to host "The New Hollywood Squares."

> *John Javna*
> The Best of TV Sitcoms
> *(1988)*

Bette Davis (1908–89)

Bette and I are very good friends. There's nothing I wouldn't say to her face—both of them.

> *Tallulah Bankhead (1950)*

Her figure was more mandolin than guitar.

Janet Flanner (1979)

She got most of her exercise by putting her foot down.

Tom Shales
Washington Post *(1989)*

Of Human Bondage (1934)—A totally obtuse concoction, serving only to demonstrate how untalented an actress Bette Davis was before she perfected those camp mannerisms.

John Simon (1967)

Daniel Day-Lewis (b 1957)
The Age of Innocence (1993)—I assume that Day-Lewis goes through the movie murmuring . . . because [director] Scorsese told him to. He recites his lines as if they'd been learned by rote in a foreign language.

Stuart Klawans
New Republic

The Last of the Mohicans (1992)—I wonder whether a dislike of Daniel Day-Lewis is genetically determined. Certainly, a dislike of James Fenimore Cooper must be.

S. J. Taylor
London Evening Standard
(1993)

James Dean (1931–55)

Mr. Dean appears to be wearing my last year's wardrobe and using my last year's talent.

Marlon Brando (1955)

Ellen DeGeneres (b 1958)

Ellen Degenerate.

Jerry Falwell
"Oprah" (1997)

[*Ellen later replied:* Nice, coming from a minister. That's what the Lord's work is, name-calling.]

"Ellen" (1997)—Ms. DeGeneres received an Emmy nomination for best actress in a comedy this year. Now, Ellen DeGeneres is a very talented comic and probably a very nice person, and I wish her nothing but the best in all her endeavors, but slap her in a sitcom and it's twenty-two minutes of her playing herself doing her stand-up routine. Which can be many things—amusing, mildly entertaining, bland, inconsequential—but "award-worthy acting" ain't one of them.

Philip Michaels

Robert De Niro (b 1943)

After appearing with DeNiro on "Saturday Night Live" (1997)—He was a bit too old and doddery for me.

Melanie Brown
(of the Spice Girls)

I can never recognize him from one movie to the
next, so I never know who he is. To me he's just an
invisible man. He doesn't exist.

Truman Capote

Robert De Niro is about as street as George Bush.

Michael Medved

Night and the City (1993)—It's a horribly hammy
performance—a grotesque parody of all his Scorsese
roles. It's Method without reason—he seems to be
thinking if he acts hard enough, everything will
suddenly make sense.

Chris Savage
Modern Review

Midnight Run (1988)—De Niro proving surprisingly
inept at milking laughs from the script. As a comedian
he relies too much on mugging and pulling faces.

Alan Stanbrook

Cape Fear (1991)—De Niro's psychotics used to nail
you to your seat; now they make you want to hide
under it.

Steve Vineberg
Modern Review *(1994)*

Cape Fear (1991)—Robert De Niro rolls through the
film like a demented descendant of Popeye the sailor.

Virgin Film Guide

Gerard Depardieu (b 1948)

Because he's French he's a sex symbol. If he was
English he'd be a dinner lady.

Donna McPhail (1994)

Bo Derek (b 1957)

Bolero (1984)—The curvaceous Bo Derek comes off as
erotically as a Dresden doll.

Motion Picture Guide

Marlene Dietrich (1901–92)

The Flame of New Orleans (1941)—Like meringue, its
sickly sweetness hurt your back teeth.

Maria Riva
(Dietrich's daughter)
Marlene Dietrich *(biography)*
(1992)

Her career was a prolonged act of audacity.

Wilfrid Sheed
New York Times *(1992)*

Phyllis Diller (b 1917)

I treasure every moment that I do not see her.

Oscar Levant

Kirk Douglas (b 1916)

Young Man with a Horn (1950)—The film I made with Kirk was one of the few utterly joyless experiences I had in films.

Doris Day

Boastful, egotistical, resentful of criticism—if anyone dare give it.

Joan Fontaine

Spartacus (1960)—In his most famous role, as the gladiator Spartacus, he had such spindly legs that he couldn't happily have carried the whole script for the epic by himself, let alone take on the whole of Rome.

Peter Tory (1992)

Roma Downey (b 1964)

"Touched by an Angel" (1997)—We can't even sit through ten minutes of "Touched by an Angel" without going into insulin shock, and somehow, we suspect Downey's sugary, vacuous performance is to blame.

The Vidiots

Fran Drescher (b 1957)

A Queens hairdresser with an accent the size of Long Island.

David Firestone
New York Times *(1994)*

Reviewing "Jenny" (1997)—Heather Paige Kent, as Maggie . . . comes across like a would-be Fran Drescher, and one Fran Drescher is plenty.

Tom Shales
Washington Post

Sonia Dresdel (1909–76)

Doctor Jo (1956)—This is a character study worthy of Joan Crawford; an antiseptic, overdressed, malarial virgin who acquired, in one of my more frivolous nightmares, the nickname of Boofy Schweitzer.

Kenneth Tynan

Keir Dullea (b 1936)

On his costar during filming for Bunny Lake Is Missing (1965)—Keir Dullea and gone tomorrow.

Noël Coward

Faye Dunaway (b 1941)

After directing Dunaway in Chinatown (1974)—She was a gigantic pain in the ass. She demonstrated certifiable proof of insanity.

Roman Polanski

Sheena Easton (b 1959)
As Aldonza in Kiss of the Spider Woman (1991)—
There's too little dirt in this Aldonza, her burnished
hair carefully combed and her well-scrubbed face
suggesting not a trollop dwelling in the lower depths
but a bratty kid doing her best to imitate an alley cat.

Anonymous Broadway critic

Clint Eastwood (b 1930)
Screen test report—You have a chip on your tooth, your
Adam's apple sticks out too far, and you talk too slow.

*Anonymous Universal Pictures
executive (1959)*

Heartbreak Ridge (1986)—Now looking increasingly
like an Easter Island statue, he has a voice pickled in
bourbon, a tongue like a razor wire, and a body so full
of shrapnel he can't walk through airport metal
detectors.

Time Out

Nelson Eddy (1901–67) **and Jeanette MacDonald**
(1907–65)
The singing capon and the iron butterfly.

Anonymous

Edith Evans (1888–1976)
She took her curtain calls as though she had just been un-nailed from the cross.

Noël Coward
Diary *(1964)*

Linda Evans (b 1942)
She has all the emotion of a goalpost.

Anonymous

Douglas Fairbanks, Jr. (b 1909)
To a woman who asked him, "Do you remember me, I met you with Douglas Fairbanks?"—Madam, I don't even remember Douglas Fairbanks!

Noël Coward

Charlie Farrell
A guy so full of himself that you could barely stand to be in the same room with him, let alone watch him on TV for half an hour. Honestly, someone must have owed him a favor.

Jack Mingo

"The Charlie Farrell Show"—It was the kind of show you watched because it was opposite Gorgeous George doing wrestling—although George was a lot funnier than Charlie Farrell.

Bill Musselwhite
Calgary Herald

Farrah Fawcett (b 1947)

On losing her train of thought while being interviewed on "The Late Show" (1997)—I'm so Farrah right now, I just lost my mind.

Janeane Garofolo

The fifty-year-old sex symbol will be featured in a nude pictorial. It's like the erotic version of the senior tour.

Jim Mullen
Entertainment Weekly (1997)

Henry Fonda (1905–82)

The Cheyenne Social Club (1970)—Costarring Shirley Jones and Rigor Mortis [Fonda], who enters early and stays through the very last scene.

Rex Reed

Jodie Foster (b 1962)

The Accused (1988)—For Jodie Foster, acting bad may be synonymous with bad acting. . . . she's breezily overemphatic, packaging herself as a babe in every sequence.

J. Hoberman
Village Voice

Michael J. Fox (b 1961)

On Fox's suitability for "Family Ties"—The kid's good, but can you see his face on a lunch box?

Brandon Tartikoff

Soleil Moon Frye (b 1976)

"Punky Brewster"—She is one of the best cases you could make about why minors should never be allowed to perform on television.

David Bianculli
New York Post

Clark Gable (1901–60)

On Gable's nickname, the "King of Hollywood"—If Clark had an inch less he'd be called the Queen of Hollywood.

Carole Lombard

Zsa Zsa Gabor (b 1919)

I have stopped swearing. I now just say "Zsa Zsa Gabor!"

Noël Coward

When he was the twenty-fourth speaker at a political dinner—I feel a little like Zsa Zsa Gabor's fifth husband. I know what I'm supposed to do, but I'm not sure how to make it interesting.

Al Gore

Greta Garbo (1905–90)

Dry and drafty, like an abandoned temple.

Truman Capote

Judy Garland (1922–69)
I didn't know her well, but after watching her in
action I didn't want to know her well.

Joan Crawford

A character ruled by petulance.

Anita Loos

Richard Gere (b 1949)
Breathless (1983)—They should have called it *Penisless.*

Howard Stern

Sommersby (1993)—Richard Gere, whose facial
expression runs the gamut from smug to smarmy.

Virgin Film Guide

John Gilbert (1897–1936)
During filming of La Boheme (1926)—Oh, no! I've got
to go through another day kissing John Gilbert.

Lillian Gish

(Sir) Alec Guinness (b 1914)
Hitler: the Last Ten Days (1973)—There are times when
Guinness's Hitler reminded me most of Jack Benny.

Vincent Canby
New York Times

Incident at Vichy (1966)—Guinness plays it like a garrulous middle-aged Galahad presenting the Grail on Prize Day at Camelot.

New Statesman

Kadeem Hardison
"Between Brothers" (1997)—Yet another triumph for the all-time champion of banal sitcom setups, Kadeem Hardison.

Peter Ko

Jean Harlow (1911–37)
Screen-testing for Hell's Angels (1930)—My God! She's got a shape like a dustpan.

Joseph March

Rex Harrison (1908–90)
My Fair Lady (1964)—Harrison is mechanically expert, like a graduate with honors from the Lord Olivier School of Going-Through-the-Motions.

Virgin Film Guide

Goldie Hawn (b 1945)
Bird on a Wire (1990)—The forty-six-year-old Goldie Hawn, supposedly playing a high-powered, successful lawyer, screams and gibbers like a twelve-year-old . . . with a spider down her back.

Christopher Tookey

Death Becomes Her (1992)—Hawn emotes like a Barbie doll on coke.

> *Alexander Walker*
> London Evening Standard

An idiot giggle, a remorseless inclination to squeak, and if a brain hummed behind those dumbfounded eyes, the secret never leaked out.

> *Donald Zec*

Helen Hayes (1900–93)

On Hayes's not being present to collect her Oscar for Airport—Helen Hayes being absent spared her—and us—one of those worthy, embarrassing standing ovations for a performance that was, let's face it, just a teensy-weensy bit terrible.

> *Vincent Canby*
> New York Times

Audrey Hepburn (1929–93)

After filming Sabrina—She's all right if you don't mind a dozen takes.

> *Humphrey Bogart*

Katharine Hepburn (b 1907) and Spencer Tracy (1900–67)

The Desk Set (1957)—They lope through this trifling charade like a couple of old-timers who enjoy reminiscing with simple routines.

> *Bosley Crowther*
> New York Times

Charlton Heston (b 1924)

Playing the stage role of a doctor—It makes me want to call out, "Is there an apple in the house?"

C. A. Lejeune

Charlton Heston, who is as big and gunny as John Wayne, but a little less legendary.

Paul Morley
Esquire *(1997)*

Earthquake (1974)—Any movie in which Charlton Heston drowns in a sewer is all right by me.

Time Out

Bill Hicks (1961–94)

Relentless (1992)—Hicks doesn't tell gags, he is an "attitude comic." Trouble is his attitude is so '60s he ought to be wearing a caftan and cowbells.

Garry Bushell

Benny Hill (1925–92)

Benny Hill has been compared to Buster Keaton, but seventy years on, Keaton comes up fresh, while Hill's forty-year-old peep show looks hopelessly outdated in a groin-and-bear-it age.

Allison Pearson

Hill's biggest defect was surely not his sexism, but the fact that he repeated himself ad nauseam.

Christopher Tookey

Judd Hirsch (b 1935)

"Taxi" (1978)—Vivacious isn't exactly the word for Hirsch, who looks like a candidate for Glummest Living American, with his air of round-shouldered defeat and a blunt, homely puss that barely supports one facial expression.

Robert Mackenzie
TV Guide

"George and Leo" (1997)—Hirsch plays a Jewish stereotype only slightly less offensive than his shameful performance in the movie *Independence Day* last year.

Tom Shales
Washington Post *(1997)*

Dustin Hoffman (b 1937)

Rain Man (1988)—Dustin Hoffman humping one note on a piano for two hours and eleven minutes.

Pauline Kael

Hook (1992)—Rathbone and Fairbanks used to fence as a natural flourish of freedom; Dustin Hoffman looks as if he learnt fencing from a correspondence course. What we get is Terry-Thomas posing for Van Dyck.

Anthony Lane

Journey of the Fifth Horse—He resembles both Sonny and Cher.

New York Daily News

During the filming of Marathon Man (1976)—Why doesn't the boy just act? Why must he go through all this Sturm und Drang?

Laurence Olivier

On being Oscar nominated as best director for Tootsie (1982)—I'd give it up, if I could have back the nine months of my life I spent with Dustin making it.

Sydney Pollack

Bob Hope (b 1903)
He's an applause junkie. Instead of growing old gracefully and doing something with his money, all he does is have an anniversary with the president looking on. He's a pathetic guy.

Marlon Brando

Anthony Hopkins (b 1941)
Coriolanus (1971)—Dressed like a cross between a fisherman and an S.S. man, evoking doggedly a Welsh rugby captain at odds with his supporters' club.

Anonymous

Magic (1978)—The gloomily withdrawn Hopkins has no vulgarity in his soul—nothing that suggests any connection with the world of entertainment—and the picture grinds along.

New Yorker

Miriam Hopkins (1902–72)
The least desirable companion on a desert island.

Harvard Lampoon *(1940)*

Bob Hoskins (b 1942)
The Inner Circle (1992)—Hoskins cameos as a leery Beria. He needn't have bothered. He contributes nothing to the movie save a "star" name.

David Aldridge
Film Review

A testicle with legs.

Pauline Kael

Rock Hudson (1925–85)
During filming of Darling Lili (1970)—Remember, *I'm* the leading lady.

Julie Andrews

Ross Hunter (1921–96)
To lambast a Ross Hunter production is like flogging a sponge.

Pauline Kael

John Hurt (b 1940)

1984 (1984)—As usual he looked just like Joan of
Arc—after she's burnt at the stake.

Anonymous

William Hurt (b 1950)

The Doctor (1992)—An ironically anemic performance
from William Hurt, who's fast becoming the big
screen's blandest man.

David Aldridge
Film Review

Wilfrid Hyde-White

Not in the Book (1958)—Precise, half-desiccated and
very wary, Wilfrid Hyde-White prowls around the
stage in search of laughs with all the blank
singlemindedness of a tortoise on a lettuce hunt.

Anonymous

Eric Idle (b 1943)

Missing Pieces (1992)—Eric Idle just calls to mind a
preschool show-off on amphetamines.

James Cameron-Wilson
Film Review

Jeremy Irons (b 1948)

The House of Spirits (1994)—I really couldn't figure out exactly what kind of accent Jeremy Irons was trying to conjure up. He was so clearly struggling with it that it seems his entire dialogue was dubbed—by Kevin Costner.

> *Rod Lurie*
> Los Angeles *magazine*

Glenda Jackson (b 1936)

An actress of some talent, whose entire persona, however, is made up of contempt and even hatred for the audience. In almost every play or film she inflicts her naked body on us, which, considering its quality, is the supreme insult flung at the spectators.

> *John Simon*

The Music Lovers (1970)—I watched *The Music Lovers.* One can't really blame Tchaikovsky for preferring boys. Anyone might become a homosexualist who had once seen Glenda Jackson naked.

> *Auberon Waugh*
> Private Eye *(1981)*

LaToya Jackson (b 1956)

An inexpressive face and a pinched little voice drained of emotion.

> *Agnes Dalbard*
> Le Parisien *(1992)*

Mick Jagger (b 1943)

Freejack (1992)—Resembling a skinny ballerina in a role more suited to Arnie, Sly, or Clint, he ignores acting by spraying the audience with lots of cod-cockney 'allos and awrights instead. Looking like he has swallowed the A–Z of acting before appearing on camera, he probably had each monosyllabic grunt engraved on his cufflinks.

John Marriott

Freejack (1992)—A strangely accented Mick Jagger makes it plain his acting career ended with *Performance* in 1970.

George Perry
The Times *of London*

Don Johnson (b 1950)

He wins the Eddie Murphy prize for milking celebrity as far as it will go.

Helen Fitzgerald

James Earl Jones (b 1931)

Othello (1982)—His Shakespearean acting has tended to be a plunge into capital-P Poetry, without much deep understanding or technical refinement, with easy reliance on his physical attributes and with much roaring.

Stanley Kauffmann
Saturday Review

Sam Jones (b 1954)
Flash Gordon (1980)—Jones in the title role has even less thespic range than Buster Crabbe showed in the old Saturday matinee cliffhangers.

Variety

Carol Kane (b 1952)
Dog Day Afternoon (1975)—Carol Kane once again proves one of our screen's most untalented and graceless presences.

John Simon

Diane Keaton (b 1946)
The Godfather, Part III (1990)—We can only be grateful that Diane Keaton is not on screen any more than she is.

Stanley Kauffmann
New Republic

Michael Keaton (b 1951)
The Paper (1994)—Keaton is becoming a worry; he may have named himself after Diane Keaton, but he's starting to act a lot more like Buster.

Julie Burchill
The Times *of London*

Grace Kelly (1929–82)

High Society (1956)—Grace Kelly gives a slightly strained performance with some unsuccessful sorties into [Katharine] Hepburn territory.

Monthly Film Bulletin

Sally Kirkland (b 1944)

I saw Sally-what's-her-name . . . that slut actress?

Judy Tenuta

Kevin Kline (b 1947)

In and Out (1997)—If you want to see Kevin Kline acting like Robin Williams acting like a stereotypical gay, this movie is for you. However, if you like intelligent comedy, it is not!

Ulrich Sondermann

Don Knotts (b 1924)

The Love God? (1969)—Strictly for the admirers of Don Knotts. Can there really be many?

Monthly Film Bulletin

Kris Kristofferson (b 1936)

A Star Is Born (1976)—Kristofferson looked like the werewolf of London stoned on cocaine and sounded like a dying buffalo.

Rex Reed

Christine Lahti (b 1950)

"Chicago Hope" (1997)—An Oscar winner, an Emmy nominee*, and by all appearances, a proud graduate of the Shannen Doherty School of Acting. No line is too simple, no comment too banal, no scene too mundane for Lahti to act as though her character bears the weight of the world. If overacting is a sin, then Lahti may one day find herself in the Ninth Circle of Hell, buried up to her neck in shit alongside a hoo-haaa-ing Al Pacino.

The Vidiots

[*For her performance she won an Emmy in 1998.]

Christopher Lambert (b 1957)

Fortress (1994)—Lambert looks distressingly like a cross between Ben Turpin and Jean-Paul Belmondo.

Philip French

Jessica Lange (b 1949)

She says she wants "mother," not "actress," on her tombstone—and I for one hope she gets it, the sooner the better. In recent years, she has developed into one of the cinema's most overrated actresses with little but a nonspecific luminosity to recommend her.

Julie Burchill
The Tatler *(1993)*

Charles Laughton (1899–1962)
He is a disappointed narcissist.

Simon Callow

King Lear (1959)—As Lear, it was one of the oddest we have seen. . . . Laughton makes no attempt to capture grandeur or majesty. His snow-white hair and beard form an almost complete circle round a pudgy face of the utmost benignity, giving him the air of an innocent Father Christmas.

Eric Keown
Punch

A Midsummer Night's Dream (1959)—He behaves throughout in a manner that has nothing to do with acting, although it perfectly hits off the demeanor of a rapscallion uncle dressed up to entertain the children at a Christmas party.

Kenneth Tynan

Sharon Lawrence (b 1962)
"Fired Up" (1997)—If we want to see acting this broad, we'll go to the nearest dinner theater.

Entertainment Weekly

"Fired Up" (1997)—Lawrence kicked comedic nuance until it was black and blue, thumbed her nose at subtlety, and pissed on the corpse of funny. And those were her better moments. At her worst, with the bad throttle slammed wide open, Lawrence's hammy posturing and jackhammer delivery reawoke long-suppressed memories of MTV irritant Jenny McCarthy.

The Vidiots

Christopher Lee (b 1922)
End of the World (1977)—Another step downwards for Christopher Lee, who had better start watching his step.

Cinefantastique

Vivien Leigh (1913–67)
Gone with the Wind (1939)—Miss Leigh gives a performance compact of vivacity, coquettishness, and rigid egoism: extremely clever and well-trained, and almost entirely without interest.

Dilys Powell

Téa Leoni (b 1966)
If we need someone to play breathy, Téa's our gal.

The Vidiots (1997)

Jerry Lewis (b 1926)
Ladies' Man (1961)—Regression into infantilism cannot be carried much further than this.

Monthly Film Bulletin

Way . . . Way Out (1966)—Another chapter in the decline and fall of Jerry Lewis.

Monthly Film Bulletin

Apparently some people find him hilariously funny.

Time Out

Shari Lewis (1934–98) **and Lambchop**
Ewwww, Lambchop. How old is that sock? If I had a sock on my hand for thirty years, it'd be talking too.

Chandler Bing
(Matthew Perry), "Friends"

John Lithgow (b 1945)
"3rd Rock from the Sun" (1996)—This popular (!?) show is about a group of aliens who assume the identities of Earthlers, to report about us to the Big Giant Head back home. Well, there already is a Big Giant Head in this program, and its name is John Lithgow. . . . All Lithgow does is overact and whine.

Anonymous
Internet review

"3rd Rock from the Sun" (1996)—Lithgow comes across like an American John Cleese of "Monty Python." . . . His performance is in part a whacked-out facial ballet, mouth askew and eyes a-pop.

> *Tom Shales*
> Washington Post

Harold Lloyd (1893–1971)
Feet First (1930)—That Lloyd was a bit pressed for laughs may be guessed from the fact that he is again dangling from the front of a skyscraper.

> Variety

Sophia Loren (b 1934)
Working with her is like being bombarded by watermelons.

> *Alan Ladd*

Courtney Love (b 1964)
She wants a part in the remake of *Breakfast at Tiffany's.* She'd be better in *Lunch at Sid and Nancy's.*

> *Jim Mullen*
> Entertainment Weekly *(1996)*

Montagu Love (1877–1943)
Mr. Love's idea of playing a he-man was to extend his chest three inches and then follow it slowly across the stage.

> *Heywood Broun*

Andie MacDowell (b 1958)

Four Weddings and a Funeral (1994)—Andie MacDowell as a light comedienne is disastrous. She is not helped by having to pretend that she has fallen for someone [Hugh Grant] who looks like a chipmunk.

> *Caren Myers*
> Sight and Sound

Jenny McCarthy (b 1972)

"Jenny" (1997)—She still tends to get a tone in her voice that might be described as "ticked-off cheerleader."

> *Steve Johnson*
> Chicago Tribune

Does anyone else find disconcerting her apparent fascination with the smell of her armpits?

> *Peter Ko (1997)*

On NBC-TV's failure to win the "Monday Night Football" slot—Which means Monday night viewing includes Frank Gifford yammering on ABC, and that Jenny McCarthy thingy on NBC. So, it's official: There will be no cure for vapidness in my lifetime.

> *Steve Rosenbloom*
> Chicago Tribune *(1998)*

(Sir) Ian McKellen (b 1939)
Hamlet (1971)—The best thing about Ian McKellen's Hamlet is his curtain call.

Harold Hobson

As an actor he has always been vastly overrated. As for his tombstone, I don't give a damn what it says on it. I just think it damnable that he will go to his grave as a knight.

John Junor

Madonna (b 1958)
Desperately Seeking Susan (1985)—She's jumped right into the movie game, but I think people should learn to act first.

Rosanna Arquette

Dick Tracy (1990)—Madonna breathes little life into Breathless Mahoney.

Curtis F. Brown (1993)

I *acted* vulgar. Madonna *is* vulgar.

Marlene Dietrich

Truth or Dare (1991)—What a tramp . . . depraved shameless hussy. . . . If there was ever an emotional cripple, it is Madonna.

New York Post

Body of Evidence (1993)—Madonna has a long way, and many acting lessons, to go.

New York Post

Evita (1997)—*Evita* attempts to revive two things long thought dead: Madonna's acting career and the movie musical. For Madonna, close but no cigar.

Peter Travers
Rolling Stone

Body of Evidence (1993)—Madonna is guilty as hell. Her crime is that she just can't act, not one stitch—or stitchless.

USA Today

John Malkovich (b 1953)

Of Mice and Men (1992)—Harder still to believe is Malkovich's shamble and gape, a simian variant of Hoffman's Rain Man.

Brian Case

Of Mice and Men (1992)—There's a love affair at the center of this—between John Malkovich and his own acting technique. . . . Somewhere . . . the story of two friends on the road becomes the Malkovich acting workshop road show. . . . When Sherilyn Fenn makes her entrance, Malkovich starts rubbing his crotch. . . . That's the movie in a nutshell: even when playing opposite someone, Malkovich still plays with himself.

Tom Shone

Marla Maples (b 1963)

The Will Rogers Follies (1992)—She lives up to her name, as wooden as two trees.

> Stewart Klein
> New York Times

Steve Martin (b 1945)

Grand Canyon (1991)—Steve Martin, [playing] the producer, is in his post-Roxanne days much like his pre-Roxanne days: unbearable.

> Stanley Kauffmann

My Blue Heaven (1990)—He gives a crude performance which is about as funny as a hernia.

> Christopher Tookey

Lee Marvin (1924–87)

After filming with Marvin in The Wild One (1953)—Lee Moron.

> Marlon Brando

Groucho Marx (1895–1977)

The man was a major comedian, which is to say that he had the compassion of an icicle, the effrontery of a carnival shill, and the generosity of a pawnbroker.

> S. J. Perelman

(Sir) John Mills (b 1908)

Ryan's Daughter (1970)—Too much makeup and on too long.

Anonymous Los Angeles critic

Liza Minnelli (b 1946)

That turnipy nose overhanging a forward-gaping mouth and a hastily retreating chin. That bulbous cranium with eyes as big and as inexpressive as saucers—those are the appurtenances of a clown.

John Simon

Cabaret (1972)—Miss Minnelli cannot act any part without calling attention to how hard she is working at it, and how far she is from having worked it out. She cannot even move right . . . she rattles around gawkily and disjointedly like someone who never got over being unfeminine and unattractive.

John Simon

Robert Mitchum (1917–97)

The Winds of War (1983)—Nowadays, Mitchum doesn't so much act as point his suit at people.

Russell Davies

You're like a pay toilet, aren't you? You don't give a shit for nothing.

Howard Hughes

Marilyn Monroe (1926–62)
How to Marry a Millionaire (1953)—Talking to Marilyn Monroe is like talking to someone underwater.

> *Nunnally Johnson*
> *(screenwriter)*

Her body has gone to her head.

> *Barbara Stanwyck*

Demi Moore (b 1963)
Disclosure (1995)—Demi Moore plays Meredith Johnson as though she had a sneak preview of Linda Fiorentino in *The Last Seduction,* but turning down the voltage.

> *Lizzie Francke*
> Sight and Sound

Ghost (1990)—Moore, as the grieving girlfriend, displays the animation of a dishcloth.

> *Dominic Wells*

Roger Moore (b 1927)
For Your Eyes Only (1981)—Roger Moore fronts for a succession of stunt men with all the relaxed, lifelike charm of a foyer poster of himself.

> The Times *of London*

Zero Mostel (1915–77)

The Front (1976)—Hearing Zero Mostel speak these
days is like having him fall on you, repeatedly.

Stanley Kauffmann

Eddie Murphy (b 1961)

The word *smug* could have been invented for him.

Tom Hutchinson

After directing Murphy in Coming to America (1988)—
I have no respect for you as an actor. You f***ed me
over as a friend.

John Landis

A Hollywood Negro.

Spike Lee

Kevin Nealon (b 1953)

ABC gives a fresh start to Kevin Nealon in "Hiller &
Diller," reminding us once more how everything the
Saturday Night Live alumnus touches turns to shit.
The man actually drains comedy out of humorous
settings.

Ben Boychuk (1997)

Anthony Newley (b 1931)
Wrinkling his head and pouting in mock self-adoration, he unfalteringly kept up the hilarious pretense that his songs were immortal and that he has a divine mission to sing them.

Clive James (1980)

Once upon a Song (1992)—He has devised an evening of such mind-numbing self-indulgence one wonders why he did not pay us to attend this unabashed audition of his life. . . . Mr. Newley's fabled vibrato is so tremulous it is as if he were shaking hands with his own larynx. His appearance has taken on a hunched, even grotesque, gnomic quality.

Jack Tinker

Paul Newman (b 1925)
The Life and Times of Judge Roy Bean (1972)—The title role looks a little heavy on Paul Newman, who gets upstaged by a bear.

Sight and Sound

Olivia Newton-John (b 1947)
Xanadu (1980)—Olivia has two expressions. She used the miffed one in *Grease,* so in *Xanadu* she shows the impish one.

Ethan Morddern
The Hollywood Musical
(1981)

Jack Nicholson (b 1937)

There's a total f***ing wanker! There's a smug, loathsome bastard!

Chris Roberts (1989)

Brigitte Nielsen (b 1963)

On their marriage—I was married by a judge. I should have asked for a jury.

Sylvester Stallone

When I look at her, I see dollar signs. And when she looks at me, I think she sees the Bank of America.

Sylvester Stallone

David Niven (1910–83)

An extremely mean and deeply heartless figure.

Peter Wilkes

David Niven (1910–83) **and Shirley Temple** (b 1928)

A Kiss for Corliss (1949)—

I sometimes think that David Niven
Should not take all the parts he's given;
While of the art of Shirley Temple
I, for the moment, have had ample.

C. A. Lejeune

Chuck Norris (b 1940)
An actor whose lack of expression is so profound that
it could be mistaken for icily controlled technique.

Nicholas Lezard
The Times *of London*

Rudolf Nureyev (1939–93)
On being described as the "Nureyev of football"—Who's
Nureyev?

Jack Lambert (1976)

Farewell Tour (1991)—Rudolf is ballet awful.

London Sun *headline*

Merle Oberon (1911–79)
That Singapore streetwalker.

Marlene Dietrich

Gary Oldman (b 1958)
Romeo Is Bleeding (1994)—Oldman in a "film noir"
means just what you'd expect: dirty white shirts, cheap
suits in need of a press, three-day growth, a bad
haircut, and a New Yawk accent and demeanor that
plays as if William Bendix had been seized with a
sudden urge to become John Garfield.

Charles Taylor
Modern Review

Michael Oliver

Problem Child 2 (1992)—No kidding, micro-monster Michael Oliver, who stars, and who in the first film ran the gamut of emotions from A to just after it, here doesn't even move from A.

> *David Aldridge*
> Film Review

(Sir) Laurence Olivier (1907–89)

Mr. Olivier does not speak poetry badly; he does not speak it at all.

> *James Agate*

Othello (1964)—There is a kind of bad acting of which only a great actor is capable. I find Sir Laurence Olivier's Othello the most prodigious and perverse example of this in a decade.

> *Alan Brien*

Romeo and Juliet (1940)—Gulping down his lines as if they were so many bad oysters.

> *John Mason Brown*
> New York Post

Olivier brandished his technique like a kind of stylistic alibi. In catching the eye, he frequently disengaged the brain.

> *Russell Davies*
> J'Accuse

Peter O'Toole (b 1932)

Macbeth (1980)—His performance suggests that he is taking some kind of personal revenge on the play.

Robert Cushman

Macbeth (1980)—He delivers every line with a monotonous tenor bark as if addressing an audience of Eskimos who have never heard of Shakespeare.

The London Guardian

Our Song (1992)—The spectacular miscasting of O'Toole as a sexual obsessive given over to a brunette half his age, when the only thing this actor seems to give himself over to is the sound of his own voice.

Matt Wolf
Variety

Jack Palance (b 1919)

Che! (1969)—Jack Palance plays Fidel Castro like a comedy act on "The Ed Sullivan Show."

Rex Reed

Jason Patric (b 1966)

Sleepers (1996)—Jason Patric's blandness in the lead role suggests he can only be "promising" for so long.

Phil Riley
Monthly Film Bulletin

Gregory Peck (b 1916)

The Sea Wolves (1980)—Peck's a Britisher in this one, but the affected accent won't fool anyone.

Variety

Sean Penn (b 1960)

After her husband, Timothy Hutton, had confided in his buddy—Having Sean Penn as a marriage counselor is like taking sailing lessons from the captain of the *Titanic.*

Debra Winger

Lori Petty (b 1964)

"Lush Life" (1996)—Better Lori Petty in *Tank Girl* for one night than "Lush Life" for twenty-two. Some sacrifices have to be made.

Ben Boychuk

Tank Girl (1995)—Lori Petty as Tank Girl . . . comes off as a valley girl rebelling against middle-class parents by shopping in a thrift shop.

Leslie Felperin
Sight and Sound

Who just by virtue of her existence is a candidate for eternal damnation.

The Vidiots (1997)

Mary Pickford (1893–1979)
She was the girl every man wanted to have—as a sister.

Alistair Cooke

Christine Pickles (b 1940)
The Misanthrope (1968)—Her Celimene is nothing more than a series of prestissimo crepitations, an unending stream of verbiage trailing behind her like a hysterically unwound roll of toilet paper.

John Simon

Ezio Pinza (1892–1957)
Bonino—Bonino? Are you sure that's not a cheap wine? Ezio . . . he was really a wooden Indian.

Tom Shales
Washington Post

Brad Pitt (b 1963)
The Devil's Own (1997)—Pitt's Irish accent was definitely the devil's own.

Dessen Howe
Washington Post *(1998)*

Legends of the Fall (1994)—A performer with more charisma than intelligence.

Virgin Film Guide

Donald Pleasence (1919–95)

Henry VII and His Six Wives (1973)—Donald Pleasence overdoes his meaching rodent act as Thomas Cromwell; the twanging Northern accent that issues from his pleated lips seems more appropriate to Dickens.

Nora Sayre
New York Times

The Merchant of Venice (1953)—I cannot imagine what Donald Pleasence was trying to make of Lancelot Gobbo, who is not, I suggest, an organ grinder's monkey.

Kenneth Tynan

Vincent Price (1911–93)

Darling of the Day (1968)—His self-congratulatory chuckles could be sold as candy in the foyer.

Walter Kerr
New York Times

Charlotte Rampling (b 1945)

A poor actress who mistakes creepiness for sensuality.

John Simon

Orca: Killer Whale (1977)—Miss Rampling is caught on the ice floes, leaping from one to t'other and clad in thigh boots, homespun poncho, and a turban, as if she expected David Bailey to surface and photograph her for *Vogue*'s Arctic number.

Alexander Walker
London Evening Standard

Nancy Reagan
The Next Voice You Hear (1950)—She projected all the passion of a Good Humor ice cream: frozen, on a stick, and all vanilla.

Spencer Tracy

Ronald Reagan (b 1911)
I can't stand the sight of Ronald Reagan. I'd like to stick my Oscar up his ass.

Gloria Grahame

Robert Redford (b 1937)
Well at least he has finally found his true love . . . what a pity he can't marry himself.

Frank Sinatra

Oliver Reed (b 1938)
His face looks like moldy melon with a half-eaten carrot for a nose and topped by a used Brillo pad.

Variety *(1980)*

Paul Reiser (b 1957)
"Mad About You" (1997)—Always the weak link in this two-link chain.

The Vidiots

Burt Reynolds (b 1936)
"Evening Shade" (1992)—This show's sickly sweet, and Burt Reynolds lives up to his character's name: Wood Newton.

Charles Catchpole

Sir Ralph Richardson (1902–83)
His voice is something between bland and grandiose: blandiose perhaps.

Kenneth Tynan

John Ritter (b 1948)
"Three's Company"—When he somehow managed to win an Emmy for best actor in a comedy in 1983, he looked as amazed as everyone else.

John Javna
The Best of TV Sitcoms
(1988)

Joan Rivers (b 1933)
When it comes to acting, Joan Rivers has the range of a wart.

Stewart Klein

Julia Roberts (b 1967)
Pretty Woman (1990)—An actress of considerable shallowness.

Virgin Film Guide

Jay Robinson
Buy Me Blue Ribbons (1951)—Mr. Robinson was game all right. But what is gameness in a man suffering from delusions of adequacy?

Walter Kerr

Dennis Rodman (b 1964)
If Dennis was on fire, he couldn't act as if he were burning. Rodman can't outact me on the big screen.

Shaquille O'Neal
"CBS Sportsline" (1997)

Mickey Rooney (b 1920)
Sugar Babies (1980)—He's a skilled technician without a dram of warmth.

Stanley Kauffmann
Saturday Review

Roseanne (b 1952)
Roseanne Barr is a bowling ball looking for an alley.

Mr. Blackwell

The closest thing to Roseanne Barr's singing the national anthem was my cat being neutered.

Johnny Carson

Richard Roundtree (b 1942)

Shaft in Africa (1973)—As an African tribesman, he looks about as indigenous as, say, during the 1930s heyday of filmed colonialism, Ralph Richardson might have looked if gotten up in blackface to infiltrate the Fuzzy Wuzzies.

Roger Greenspun
New York Times

Meg Ryan (b 1961)

Sleepless in Seattle (1993)—Doris Day meets Cosmo Girl at the therapist.

Julie Burchill
The Times *of London*

Rob Schneider (b 1965)

"Men Behaving Badly" (1997)—One of the most annoying actors on television . . . as the star of the show he just grates. He's a '90s Squiggy—and there's a reason why Squiggy never got his own spinoff.

Bruce Fretts
Entertainment Weekly

Arnold Schwarzenegger (b 1947)

Arnold is an arch manipulator, an incorrigible womanizer, a hypocrite, and a control freak, a man with a cruel streak who cannot admit to an iota of weakness.

*Anonymous Hollywood
producer*

Arnold Schwarzenegger looks like a condom full of walnuts.

Clive James

Red Heat (1988)—At the end, Schwarzenegger makes his ritual progress for the climactic showdown, decking himself out in leather, packing up an arsenal of guns, and, as he leaves his apartment, copping a quick look of satisfaction in the mirror. It is his only love scene.

Pauline Kael
Hooked *(1989)*

Eraser (1996)—Arnold tests his acting ability and fails. . . . *Eraser* demands a solid, dramatic performance from the star, something he is incapable of giving.

Eric Monder
Monthly Film Bulletin

Playing Mr. Freeze in Batman and Robin (1997)—It's an odd day in Tinseltown when Schwarzenegger in sci-fi makeup is less exciting than a TV actor ["ER"'s George Clooney as Batman] who does battle in tights. But as they say in the comics, that's charisma, baby. When you're hot you're hot, and when you're not, you're a frozen stiff.

Liza Schwarzbaum
Entertainment Weekly

Paul Scofield (b 1922)

Othello (1980)—His idea of a black man's movements consisted of a kind of Fairbankian prancing which, in moments of deep anguish, came to resemble an orangutan choreographed by Sir Frederick Ashton.

Peter Jenkins
The Spectator

George C. Scott (b 1927)

The Little Foxes (1967)—His diction is really too sloppy for a leading actor in anything but a theater for convalescent throat patients.

John Simon

Steven Seagal (b 1951)

And if you can make a star out of Steven Seagal, you can make a star out of anyone.

Mike Bygrave

Under Siege (1993)—Bring back Bruce Willis . . . at least he's funny.

Colette Maude

Jerry Seinfeld (b 1954)

F*** him and his tired Jewish New York humor.

Arena *(1998)*

Tom Selleck (b 1945)

Carry On, Columbus (1992)—A miscast Tom Selleck, as a petulant King Ferdinand, complete with Prince Valiant wig, is a Magnum farce.

David Aldridge
Film Review

Peter Sellers (1925–80)

The Mouse That Roared (1959)—Engaging science fiction satire—marred somewhat by Sellers' determination to be a second-league Alec Guinness.

Alan Frank
Science Fiction Handbook
(1982)

Omar Sharif (b 1932)

Che! (1969)—Omar Sharif can no more interpret the fiery revolutionary [Che Guevara] than Elvis Presley could portray Lenin.

Sherwood Ross

William Shatner (b 1931)

Double Play (1996)—The plump Shatner mesmerizes. . . . Too bad the only double he has is a chin.

Joe Neumaier
Entertainment Weekly *(1997)*

Norma Shearer (1900–83)

The Women (1939)—I love to play bitches, and Norma Shearer certainly helped me in this part.

Joan Crawford

Cybill Shepherd (b 1949)

At Long Last Love (1975)—Cybill Shepherd is a leading lady who can neither sing nor dance, and who apparently thinks badinage is something you put on a small cut.

Vincent Canby
New York Times

At Long Last Love (1975)—A poor star gives the most atrocious performance in musical history. She's supposed to charm; why is she angry and pushy?

Ethan Morddern
The Hollywood Musical
(1981)

Anthony Sher (b 1949)

Twelfth Night (1987)—He plays Malvolio like Groucho Marx dressed as a Greek none-too-orthodox priest.

Sheridan Morley

Brooke Shields (b 1965)

"Suddenly Susan" (1997)—That's quite some feat she pulled off, getting acted off the screen by Judd Nelson.

The Vidiots

The Russians love Brooke Shields because her
eyebrows remind them of Leonid Brezhnev.

Robin Williams

Dinah Shore (1917–94)
Watching Dinah Shore for just one week is like being
imprisoned inside a giant butterscotch sundae.

Harry Walters
Newsweek

Simone Signoret (1921–85)
Macbeth (1966)—Simone Signoret's Lady Macbeth was
in need of both subtitles and microphones.

Thomas Curtiss
New York Times

Jay Silverheels (1919–80)
The Man Who Loved Cat Dancing (1973)—Even the
Indians looked fake, including good old Jay Silverheels,
who is real.

Roger Greenspun
New York Times

Jonathan Silverman (b 1966)
"The Single Guy" (1995)—He has gone from being
the Triple A Matthew Broderick to being an
adequately menschy David Schwimmer.

David Wild
Rolling Stone

Christian Slater (b 1969)

Heathers (1989)—I wish it wasn't quite so obvious that his acting hero is Jack Nicholson.

Christopher Tookey

William Squire

The Elder Statesman (1958)—William Squire prances and cavorts like a refugee from a horror film in which Peter Lorre was filling in for Boris Karloff.

Alan Brien
The Spectator

Sylvester Stallone (b 1946)

Escape to Victory (1981)—A soccer film set in a POW camp, it features actors who can't play soccer (Michael Caine), soccer players who can't act (Pele), and Americans who can do neither (Stallone).

Nick Hornby
The Times *of London*

Rod Steiger (b 1925)

The Illustrated Man (1968)—It is not enough for Mr. Steiger to huff, puff, and acquaint us once more with his impressive set of mannerisms.

Saturday Review

Oklahoma! (1955)—Rod Steiger sticks out like a sore Method actor.

Mike Summer (1994)

Marti Stevens

High Spirits (1964) [the non-Coward musical adaptation
of *Blithe Spirit*]—I'm very proud of you. You managed
to play the first act of my little comedy tonight with
all the Chinese flair and lighthearted brilliance of Lady
Macbeth.

Noël Coward

Geoffrey Steyne

Mr. Steyne's performance was the worst to be seen in
the contemporary theater.

Heywood Broun (1917)

[*Steyne sued Broun for libel,
prompting the critic to review (sub
judice) the plaintiff's next stage
appearance*—Mr. Steyne's
performance is not up to his
usual standard.]

Sharon Stone (b 1958)

It's a new low for actresses when you have to wonder
what's between her ears instead of her legs.

Katharine Hepburn

After the flop of *Sliver*, get back to basics. Remember,
we don't all "like to look." Do penance for losing your
knickers: wear wool next to the skin.

Alexander Walker
London Evening Standard
(1993)

Meryl Streep (b 1949)

Recounting his career as a film critic—I suspect that at least 10 percent of my time in the auditorium was spent with one hand across my eye—although this was often at the sight of Meryl Streep, rather than any more ostensible horror.

> Peter Ackroyd
> The Spectator *(1987)*

Despite her almost Nordic looks, she comes across like a bleached Jewish mother with a tongue to match.

> Bob Flynn

Meryl Streep just about always seems miscast. She makes a career out of seeming to overcome being miscast.

> Pauline Kael

Out of Africa (1985)—She is so rarefied as to leave one cold.

> Virgin Film Guide

Barbra Streisand (b 1942)

The Way We Were (1973)—She's not really an actress, not even much of a comedienne. She's an impersonator. . . . When she goes one way and the movie goes another, it's no contest. The movie is turned to junk.

> Vincent Canby
> New York Times

What's Up, Doc? (1972)—She does her own schtick . . .
but she doesn't do anything she hasn't already done.
She's playing herself—and it's awfully soon for that.

> *Pauline Kael*
> New Yorker

A Star Is Born (1976)—Streisand looked and sounded
ridiculous trying to be Grace Slick.

> *Rex Reed*

All Night Long (1981)—Streisand makes no pretense of
acting at all. I thought I'd never seen a worse portrayal
of an allegedly living, breathing human being than
Streisand gave in *The Main Event,* but the lustful little
turnip she plays in *All Night Long* puts some of the
creatures in *Freaks* to shame.

> *Merrill Shindler*
> Los Angeles *magazine*

A Star Is Born (1976)—Gifted with a face that shuttles
between those of a tremulous young borzoi and a
fatigued Talmudic scholar. . . . O, for the gift of
Rostand's *Cyrano* to evoke the vastness of that nose as
it cleaves the giant screen from east to west, bisects it
from north to south. It zigzags across our horizon like
a bolt of fleshy lightning; it towers like a ziggurat
made of meat. The hair is now something like the wig
of a fop in Restoration comedy; the speaking voice
continues to sound like Rice Krispies if they could
talk. And Streisand's notion of acting is to bulldoze
her way from one end of a line to the other without
regard for anyone or anything; you can literally feel
her impatience for the other performer to stop talking
so she can take over again. . . . This hypertrophic ego
and bloated countenance.

> *John Simon*
> New York *magazine*

Ed Sullivan (1901–74)
Ed Sullivan will always be around as long as someone
else has talent.

> *Fred Allen*

Kiefer Sutherland (b 1966)
On Sutherland's directorial debut in Truth or
Consequences, N.M. (1997)—Sutherland the director
indulges Sutherland the actor's penchant for playing
psychopathic lowlifes. You may want to shoot yourself
rather than have to watch him wave a gun crazily at
anyone ever again.

Lisa Schwarzbaum
Entertainment Weekly

Janet Suzman (b 1939)
Antony and Cleopatra (1973)—Where Shakespeare had
written the word "O," she favored us with an
extended imitation of a hurrying ambulance.

Anonymous

Patrick Swayze (b 1954)
Ghost (1990)—Swayze, he of the acting ability of a
corpse, is ideal as the murdered yuppie.

Dominic Wells

Loretta Swit (b 1937)
Forest Warrior (1996)— . . . and a special appearance by
Loretta Swit. (Isn't that an oxymoron?)

Bruce Fretts
Entertainment Weekly

Tommy Tang
Tommy Tang's Modern Thai Cuisine (1997)—
Self-indulgent and self-centered.

> *William Rice*
> Chicago Tribune

Elizabeth Taylor (b 1932)
The queen of sequential monogamy.

> *Arianna Huffington*
> New York *magazine (1983)*

The Little Foxes (1981)—To use a camera term, Taylor
seems repeatedly to go in and out of focus during
scenes. Worse, in the climaxes, her force comes from
her throat, not her spirit; the result is only noise. A
Martian, ignorant of Taylor's film past, seeing her for
the first time here, might wonder how an actress of
her age could have developed so little technique and
could have become a star with so little ability to take
command.

> *Stanley Kauffmann*
> Saturday Review

Cleopatra (1962)—Miss Taylor is monotony in a slit
skirt, a pre-Christian Elizabeth Arden with sequined
eyelids and occasions constantly too large for her.

> New Statesman

The old girl has obviously had everything sucked out that could be sucked out, and everything lifted that could be lifted. Indeed, from her tight-skinned, sixty-year-old face and taught, little body, they must have had to take away the surplus in truckloads.

Lynda-Lee Potter
London Mail (1992)

Elizabeth Taylor's so fat, she puts mayonnaise on an aspirin.

Joan Rivers

Overweight, overbosomed, overpaid, and undertalented, she set the acting profession back a decade.

David Susskind

A vamp who destroys families and sucks on husbands like a praying mantis.

Il Tempo (1961)

Every minute this broad spends outside of bed is a waste of time.

Michael Todd

Emma Thompson (b 1959)
Why do I keep seeing all those wonderful pictures of Emma Thompson looking so lovely and so talented? I think she might have to go to the hospital soon. I think I might have to put her there.

Dawn French (1988)

On learning that Thompson's husband, Kenneth Branagh, was to direct Frankenstein—No doubt he's looking for the right person to be the monster, someone whose acting ability won't be affected by a bolt through the neck. E.T. phone home. Your husband has a job for you.

Jill Parkin

I wonder whether a dislike of Emma Thompson is genetically determined. I dislike Emma Thompson. I dislike her throaty delivery of lines—an act of bravura that seems to have been misinterpreted as acting by the many.

S. J. Taylor
London Evening Standard
(1993)

David Threlfall

As Prince Charles in Diana: Her True Story (1993)— David Threlfall at least looks like Prince Charles, even if his performance is more parody than portrayal. He speaks through clamped jaws, his mouth stretched permanently to one side, as if trying to capture something to eat at the base of his skull.

Jaci Stephens
The Times *of London*

Rip Torn (b 1931)
Desire Under the Elms (1963)—Rip Torn, playing Eben
like a refugee from a Texas lunatic asylum, giggles
when he is in despair, stares blankly when he is
unhappy, and spits when he is undecided.

Robert Brustein

Spencer Tracy (1900–67)
Dr. Jekyll and Mr. Hyde (1941)—Mr. Tracy's portrait
of Hyde is not so much evil incarnate as ham
rampant . . . more ludicrous than dreadful.

John Lee Mahin (screenwriter)
New York Times

While being shown round the studio during filming of Dr.
Jekyll and Mr. Hyde (1941)—Which part is he playing
now, Jekyll or Hyde?

W. Somerset Maugham

Chris Tucker
The Fifth Element (1997)—Tucker, nattering into a tiny
neck-mounted microphone, is like Dennis Rodman,
Little Richard, and Urkel stirred up in the same
cocktail shaker.

Owen Gleiberman
Entertainment Weekly

Kathleen Turner (b 1954)

She is her biggest fan. If Kathleen Turner had been a man, I would have punched her out long ago.

Burt Reynolds (1988)

Lana Turner (b 1920)

She is not even an actress—only a trollop.

Gloria Swanson

Jean-Claude Van Damme (b 1960)

Nowhere to Run (1993)—You can take a horse to water but you can't make him act.

James Cameron-Wilson
Film Review

He has about three moves he uses over and over in every single one of his films. He does that jump-back spin-kick, and that's pretty much all he does.

Brandon Lee (1992)

Double Impact (1992)—The Belgian martial-arts superstar always sounds like he's being dubbed from a foreign language, even though he's clearly speaking English.

Motion Picture Guide

Dick Van Dyke (b 1925)

Mary Poppins—The greatest exponent of vocal idiocy.

Jonathan Margolis

The Village People
Can't Stop the Music (1980)—They've a long way to go in the acting stakes. Some scenes one could pulp and thereby solve the world paper shortage, they're so wooden.

Variety

Monica Vitti (b 1931)
I fell in love with all my leading ladies. Oh, except Monica Vitti. No one could love Monica Vitti.

Dirk Bogarde

Ally Walker (b 1961)
"Profiler" (1997)—If it hadn't been for her crossed eyes and tilted head, someone might actually have made a bigger deal about her show being remarkably lame.

"I understand the criminal mind." Right. She understands the criminal mind like we understand hummus.

The Vidiots

Robin Williams (b 1951)
He reminds me of nothing so much as a homeless dog crazed into near dementia by the need to be petted.

Michael Atkinson
Modern Review *(1994)*

2

MOVIES

The amusing thing about moving pictures is the enormous number of nonentities who work together to make something any normal half-wit would prefer not to make in the first place.

Anonymous

Popcorn is the last area of movie business where good taste is still a concern.

Mike Barfield
The Oldie *(1992)*

Trying to write honestly about pornographic films is like trying to tie one's shoes while walking.

Vincent Canby
New York Times *(1973)*

The cinema has become more and more like the theater, it's all mauling and mumbling.

Shelagh Delaney
A Taste of Honey

I wouldn't take the advice of a lot of so-called film critics on how to shoot a closeup of a teapot.

(Sir) David Lean

Judging films should be the same as judging jokes. It's no good saying this is a wonderful joke if no one laughs at it.

Anthony Lejeune (1992)

Pearson's First Rule of Film Criticism: The further a film deviates from the critical norm—i.e., serious drama—the less reliable the criticism of it.

Harry Pearson
Films in Review *(1992)*

You get a feeling that if *The Wizard of Oz* were remade today, the yellow brick road would be brought to you courtesy of Carpeteria.

Peter Rainier
Los Angeles Herald
Examiner

Critics don't represent anyone but themselves. They don't like popular films because they don't want to associate themselves with the great unwashed. Cinema is about light relief after a hard day, not high art.

Michael Winner

HOLLYWOOD

Living in Hollywood is like living in a bowl of granola. What ain't fruits and nuts is flakes.

Anonymous

On the film version of his book The Hunt for Red October—Giving your book to Hollywood is like turning your daughter in to a pimp.

Tom Clancy

You can't find any true closeness in Hollywood. Everyone does the fake closeness so well.

Carrie Fisher

They've got great respect for the dead in Hollywood . . . but none for the living.

Errol Flynn

Hollywood may be thickly populated but to me it's a bewilderness.

Sir Cedric Hardwicke

Hollywood is a machine run by people who are serving an idea which no longer exists, never did exist, and which, in any case, is a lie.

Glenda Jackson (1969)

Hollywood is the only community in the world where the entire population is suffering from rumortism.

Bert Lahr

Hollywood always had a streak of totalitarianism in just about everything it did.

Shirley MacLaine

Hollywood is where the stars twinkle, then wrinkle.

Victor Mature

Planet Hollywood: a chain of poorly run, high-priced, inexplicably popular eateries.

Philip Michaels

Hollywood is a sunny place for shady people.

Ferenc Molnar

Hollywood is where you find a combination of hotheads and cold shoulders.

Gregory Peck

Hollywood is a piquant mixture of the Main Line, the Mermaid Tavern, and any lesser French penal colony.

S. J. Perelman

Hollywood is a town that has to be seen to be disbelieved.

Walter Winchell

THE OSCARS (ACADEMY AWARDS)

After Tristiana *was nominated for Best Foreign Movie—* Nothing would disgust me more morally than winning an Oscar. Nothing in the world would make me accept it. I wouldn't have it in my home.

Luis Buñuel
Variety *(1970)*

The Academy Awards is all politics and sentiment, and nothing to do with merit.

Truman Capote

The Oscars are some sort of masturbatory fantasy. I would rather have a good three-man basketball game than sit here in my monkey suit.

Elliott Gould

The Oscars are obscene, dirty, and grotesque, no better than a beauty contest.

Dustin Hoffman

The Oscar process is offensive, barbarous, and innately corrupt.

George C. Scott (1970)

It's insane to have winners and losers in art. To say one performance is better than another is just plain dumb. You wouldn't think of comparing two colors in a painting, would you? This blue is better than that blue?

Meryl Streep (1978)

Oscar time is the intellectual rutting season . . . a thoroughly awful and debasing time.

Dalton Trumbo

You can't eat awards . . . nor, more to the point, drink 'em.

John Wayne

DIRECTORS AND PRODUCERS

Successful directors seem to become so powerful,
through their ability to attract star actors and so on,
that they can be as self-indulgent, whimsical,
mannered, and digressive as they please. If a new film
comes along and you recognize its director's name,
think twice about going.

> *Kingsley Amis*
> The Spectator *(1985)*

There are maybe one or two good directors. The rest
are atmosphere.

> *Robert Blake*
> Esquire *(1976)*

You could spend the rest of your life explaining *The
Elephant Man* to Warner Brothers.

> *Mel Brooks (1989)*

Film directors are people too short to become actors.

> *Josh Greenfield*

Bad directors are the ones who want to control
everything.

> *Anthony Hopkins*

Hollywood producers see their job as to make the thing everyone made last year.

David Mamet (1993)

Robert Aldrich

Hustle (1975)—Even with such a meandering script as this, one expects more than the paltry fare Aldrich offers.

Paul Coleman

Hush, Hush, Sweet Charlotte (1964)—Aldrich only just manages to keep this side of being disgusting and that side of being ridiculous.

Films and Filming

Woody Allen

The only person who takes Woody Allen seriously is Woody Allen. . . . His face has the slackness of an old onion; his hair seems to fall in clumps whenever he moves; his voice, squeezed with difficulty through those grimly pursed lips, has the whine of a child screaming for more—more of everything.

Peter Ackroyd
The Spectator *(1981)*

Contrary to popular opinion, Woody Allen is not a very good filmmaker. His self-indulgent nebbishism is inorganic, pointless, coarse, and often dreary. His style is not groundbreaking, but frequently inexpressive and shabby.

Cinefantastique

On Allen's affair with Soon-Yi Previn—You couldn't print what I think. As a father I don't have a colorful enough vocabulary.

André Previn (1992)

Pedro Almodovar
Women on the Verge of a Nervous Breakdown (1988)— The best to be said for it is that Almodovar makes a good interior decorator.

Mark Finch
Monthly Film Bulletin

Robert Altman
When one hears the word "contempt," one thinks of Robert Altman.

Richard Corliss
Time

McCabe and Mrs. Miller (1971)—Altman directed "M*A*S*H," which wandered and was often funny; then *Brewster McCloud,* which wandered and was not funny; now this, which wanders and is repulsive.

Stanley Kauffmann

Michelangelo Antonioni
Zabriskie Point (1969)—He has tried to make a serious movie and hasn't even achieved a beach-party level of insight.

Roger Ebert

It seems that boredom is one of the great discoveries of our time. If so, there's no question but that he must be considered a pioneer.

Luchino Visconti

Ingmar Bergman
Persona (1966)—A characteristic piece of self-indulgence on Bergman's part—Bergman talking to himself again.

David Wilson
Monthly Film Bulletin

Luc Besson
The Big Blue (1988)—The director's future as a significant cinematic navigator looks, on this evidence, rather less than watertight.

Philip Strick
Monthly Film Bulletin

Peter Bogdanovich
Daisy Miller (1974)—Appallingly crass . . . directed with all the subtlety of a sledgehammer.

Michael Billington
Illustrated London News

Texasville (1990)—Making a hash of trying to adapt
Larry McMurtry's extremely long and dense novel,
Bogdanovich has simply thrown away all the flesh and
kept the bones.

Tom Milne
Monthly Film Bulletin

John Boorman
Excalibur (1981)—Left entirely to his own devices,
Boorman seems to run in self-defeating circles.

Richard Combs
Monthly Film Bulletin

Kenneth Branagh
Henry V (1989)—Branagh appears to see William
Shakespeare less as drama than an occasion for dazzling
solo turns.

Bruce Bawor
American Spectator

Robert Bresson
Lancelot of the Lake—The truth is that what Robert
Bresson has done to poor old King Arthur would not
have passed muster as a music hall lampoon.

Benny Green
Punch

Mel Brooks
Spaceballs (1987)—At its worst, it displays a colossal ego
at work and humor better left to home movies.

Daily Variety

High Anxiety (1977)—Brooks has no idea of how to build a sequence, how to tell a story, when to leave well enough (or ill enough) alone.

Philip French

High Anxiety (1977)—A child's idea of satire—imitations, with a comic hat and a leer.

New Yorker

Frank Capra
Mr. Deeds Goes to Town (1936)—I have an uneasy feeling he's on his way out. He's started making films about themes instead of people.

Alistair Cooke

Harry Cohn
His Crudeness.

Anonymous

He was absolutely ice cold in his self-interest.

Norman Krasna

He was the meanest man I ever knew . . . a reconstructed dinosaur.

Budd Schulberg

Kevin Costner

Dances with Wolves (1991)—This epic was made by a bland megalomaniac. The Indians should have named him "Plays with Camera."

Pauline Kael

Michael Curtiz

Life with Father (1947)—The director is totally out of his element in this careful, deadly version.

New Yorker *(1978)*

Dino De Laurentis

Flash Gordon (1980)—De Laurentis's production is a disaster. Put more simply, it's the worst outgrowth of the recent crop of lavishly produced but empty-headed genre films.

Cinefantastique

Jonathan Demme

Last Embrace (1979)—A case study of late seventies movie making which does everything in its power to avoid taking risks.

John Pym
Monthly Film Bulletin

Cecil B. DeMille

Inspirationally and imaginatively, C.B. was sterile.
His stories, situations, and characters were, almost
without exception, unintelligent, unintuitive, and
psychologically adolescent.

> *Norman Bel Geddes*
> Miracles in the Evening
> *(1960)*

Unconquered (1947)—DeMille bangs the drum as loudly
as ever but his sideshow has gone cold on us.

> *Richard Winnington*

Brian de Palma

Bonfire of the Vanities (1991)—A misfire of inanities.
This is a failure of epic proportions. You've got to be a
genius to make a movie this bad.

> *Joel Siegel*
> ABC-TV

John Derek

Bolero (1984)—Only two films in recent history come
close to rivaling this junk for stupidity and ineptitude,
and both of them just happen to have been by Derek.
They were *Tarzan: The Ape-Man* and *A Boy . . . A
Girl.* Derek could open his own turkey farm.

> Motion Picture Guide

Vittorio De Sica (1901–74)

A fine actor, a polished hack, and a flabby whore . . .
not necessarily in that order.

Stanley Kauffmann

Allan Dwan

The Most Dangerous Man Alive (1961)—Director Allan
Dwan is a cult figure in France . . . but not for this
one!

Castle of Frankenstein

Clint Eastwood

Sudden Impact (1983)—Eastwood presumably takes
credit for such gems of authorial self-awareness as
replacing the orangutan of the *Which Way* films with a
farting dog.

Paul Taylor
Monthly Film Bulletin

Blake Edwards

Skin Deep (1989)—Edwards's undeniable personal
obsessions are winding up as bland, uniform, nothing-
in-particular films like this.

Kim Newman
Monthly Film Bulletin

Nora Ephron

This Is My Life (1992)—The directing debut of screenwriter Nora Ephron. On this evidence she should stick to writing because she hasn't a clue about pace and comic timing.

Anne Billson

This Is My Life (1992)—On the evidence of her directorial debut, she should not give up her day job.

Nigel Floyd

Federico Fellini

Satyricon (1969)—Part of the gradual decomposition of what was once one of the greatest talents in film history . . . a gimcrack, shopworn nightmare.

Geoff Andrew

Menahem Golan

The Magician of Lublin (1979)—California Polish accents grapple with ham-fisted direction and a script [also cowritten by Golan] of surpassing banality.

Sight and Sound

Samuel Goldwyn

A titan with an empty skull.

Billy Wilder

Ben Hecht
Ben Hecht was two men, a skilled commercial hack
and a pretentious jerk.

Leslie Halliwell
Halliwell's Harvest *(1986)*

Amy Heckerling
Look Who's Talking Too (1990)—Whenever Heckerling
runs out of inspiration, which is every couple of
minutes, she slaps an old rock 'n' roll record on the
turntable and transforms the film into a music video.

Philip French

Alfred Hitchcock
The Birds (1963)—You cannot teach an old dog new
tricks, and as much as we respect Alfred Hitchcock, a
Hitchcock film is now as predictable as Christmas
dinner and about as indigestible.

Films and Filming

The Secret Agent (1936)—How unfortunate it is that
Mr. Hitchcock, a clever director, is allowed to produce
and even to write his own films, though as a producer
he has no sense of continuity and as a writer he has no
sense of life.

Graham Greene

Psycho (1960)—A sad prostitution of talent. . . . It's sad
to see a really big man make a fool of himself.

London Express

Psycho (1960)—A lascivious bloodbath. . . . He has become a caterer for cheap sniggers.

London Sunday Dispatch

Psycho (1960)—Merely one of those television shows padded out to two hours by adding pointless subplots and realistic detail . . . a reflection of a most unpleasant mind, a mean, sly, sadistic little mind.

Dwight Macdonald
Esquire

Psycho (1960)—Hitch, old cock . . . this is the worst film you've ever made. . . . It scrapes the bottom of the psychiatric barrel.

Fred Majdalany

Mr. and Mrs. Smith (1941)—A slight Hitch.

Time Out *(1992)*

Norman Jewison

Fiddler on the Roof (1971)—Jewison hasn't so much directed a film as prepared a product for world consumption.

Stanley Kauffmann

Stanley Kramer

Judgment at Nuremberg (1961)—Some believe that by tackling such themes Kramer earns at least partial remission from criticism. How much? Twenty percent for effort?

Stanley Kauffmann

Stanley Kubrick

The only memorable character in Kubrick's films over the past twenty years is Hal the computer.

Pauline Kael
New Yorker *(1987)*

2001: A Space Odyssey (1968)—Incredibly ponderous and languid. Kubrick plays with his model hardware like a child with a construction set—and I was on the outside not allowed in.

The London Daily Sketch

Lolita (1962)—The director's heart is apparently elsewhere.

Andrew Sarris

A Clockwork Orange (1971)—Pointless, feeble fantasy, a complete bore. . . . Kubrick tricks up his feeble continuities with the kind of speeded-up sexploitation scene that wins prizes at erotic film festivals for "humor."

Village Voice

Fritz Lang
The Secret Behind the Door (1948)—Lang gets a few wool-silky highlights out of this sow's ear, but it's a hopeless job and a worthless movie.

> James Agee

Spike Lee
Malcolm X (1992)—The message is: "Send a boy to do a man's job."

> Stanley Crouch

This is a sick little guy, a merchant of shame.

> Roy Innis (1992)

Claude Lelouch
A Man and a Woman (1966)—When in doubt, Lelouch's motto seems to be, use a color filter or insert lyrical shots of dogs and horses; when in real doubt, use both.

> Tom Milne
> Monthly Film Bulletin

George Lucas
Star Wars (1977)—Heartless fireworks ignited by a permanently retarded director with too much clout and cash.

> Time Out (1984)

Sidney Lumet

Guilty as Sin (1993)—The director is Sidney Lumet. I have absolutely no reason why he dunnit.

Derek Malcolm

Herman Mankiewicz

To know him was to like him. Not to know him was to love him.

Bert Kalmar

Joseph L. Mankiewicz

There Was a Crooked Man (1970)—Directed in the Grand Rapids style of moviemaking.

Pauline Kael
New Yorker

Garry Marshall

Pretty Woman (1990)—Marshall directs like he was wearing earplugs and boxing gloves on the set.

Virgin Film Guide

Louis B. Mayer (1885–1957)

He wore a $250 suit and was mantled in the arrogance of his own success.

Charles Bickford
Bulls, Balls, Bicycles, and
Actors *(1965)*

On Mayer's suggesting a round of golf—My boy, when I want to play with a prick, I'll play with my own.

W. C. Fields

John McTiernan

Last Action Hero (1993)—McTiernan pitches ham-fistedly at a postmodern attention span and shoots with the subtlety of a rampaging rhino. This is filmmaking of the "more-is-more" school.

Tom Charity

John Milius

Red Dawn (1983)—When is Mr. Milius going to put his toy soldiers away and grow up?

Motion Picture Guide

Dudley Nichols

Mourning Becomes Electra (1947)—Dudley Nichols must have wanted to film *Mourning Becomes Electra* very badly; he filmed it very badly indeed.

Leslie Halliwell
Halliwell's Harvest *(1986)*

Alan Parker

Angel Heart (1987)—Alan Parker has all the technique to burn in *Angel Heart,* and that's what he should have done with it.

Pauline Kael

Otto Preminger

Hurry Sundown (1967)—Preminger's taste is atrocious. His idea of erotic symbolism is Jane Fonda caressing Michael Caine's saxophone.

Cue

The Human Factor (1979)—Unfortunately, Preminger stages it all as if he was just trying to get all the actors through their line readings in under two hours, allowing no breathing room or time for character nuance in a tale which resolutely calls for quiet moments.

Variety

David Puttnam

Memphis Belle (1990)—Another chapter in Puttnam's peculiar cinema of history lessons without cinematic depth or sound dramatic portfolio.

Richard Combs
Monthly Film Bulletin

Ken Russell

Pry open Ken Russell's brain and toads would jump out.

Anonymous

Savage Messiah (1972)—No list of the most awful films of the year would be complete without something by Ken Russell.

> *Vincent Canby*
> New York Times *(1973)*

The Devils (1970)—Ken Russell doesn't report hysteria, he markets it.

> New Yorker *(1976)*

Lisztomania (1975)—This gaudy compendium of camp, secondhand Freud, and third-rate pastiche is like a bad song without end.

> Sight and Sound

The Devils (1970)— . . . the Torquemada School of Film Direction.

> *Alexander Walker*
> London Evening Standard

Martin Scorsese

Cape Fear (1992)—It not only leaves a nasty taste, it is a clumsy, less than effective thriller. Yet it does have incidental, unintended worth, by betraying how Scorsese and his peers see the world—and what sort of people they think we are. Their world is rotten, teeming with hollow men, and filmgoers are slow-witted sensation seekers who must have everything spelled out. In capital letters.

> *Shaun Usher (1992)*

Tony Scott

Beverly Hills Cop II (1987)—Scott's direction is a Mixmaster without a compass.

Brian Case

David O. Selznick

Selznick gave the impression that he stormed through life demanding to see the manager—and that, when the manager appeared, Selznick would hand him a twenty-page memo announcing his instant banishment to Elba.

Lloyd Shearer

Don Siegel

The Black Windmill (1974)—Direction as blank as the expression on Michael Caine's face throughout.

Sight and Sound

Steven Spielberg

He doesn't know anything about actors, that's for sure.

Bruce Dern
Films Illustrated *(1978)*

Close Encounters of the Third Kind: Special Edition (1980)—One is inclined to feel that with all the money [$20 million] at his disposal, Spielberg might have got it right the first time.

Derek Malcolm

Sylvester Stallone

Staying Alive (1983)—Stallone doesn't bother much with character, scenes, or dialogue. He just puts the newly muscle-plated John Travolta in front of the camera, covers him with what looks like an oil slick, and goes for wham-bams.

Pauline Kael
New Yorker

George Stevens

The Greatest Story Ever Told (1965)—George Stevens was once described as the water buffalo of film art. What this film more precisely suggests is a dinosaur.

Monthly Film Bulletin

Oliver Stone

JFK (1991)—In his three-hour lie, Stone falsifies so much he may be an intellectual sociopath.

George Will

Quentin Tarantino

Tarantino has clearly seen a lot of movies; what he hasn't seen is a lot of life.

Christopher Bray
The Times *of London (1994)*

Irving Thalberg

Irving Thalberg was a sweet guy, but he could piss ice water.

Eddie Mannix

Jean-Claude Tramont
All Night Long (1981)—A directorial style no more advanced than the type used to film baby's first tooth.

> Merrill Shindler
> Los Angeles *magazine*

Luchino Visconti
Death in Venice (1971)—A prime contender for the title of "Most Overrated Film of All Time."

> Time Out *(1985)*

Walt Disney Studios
The Holy Rodent Empire.

> Spy *(1994)*

A place where they killed you to keep you from starving to death.

> *Igor Stravinsky*

Orson Welles
Touch of Evil (1958)—Pure Orson Welles and impure balderdash, which may be the same thing.

> Gerald Weales
> Reporter

Billy Wilder
His critiques of films are subtle and can be very amusing, especially of the ones he hasn't seen.

> *David Hockney*

Darryl F. Zanuck

The only man who can eat an apple through a tennis racquet.

David Niven

Franco Zeffirelli

The Taming of the Shrew (1967)—With his misty-glow Renaissance decor, he manages to smother Shakespeare in pizza-Sennett.

Judith Crist

Hamlet (1991)—Two-plus hours in the company of Franco "one classic with everything on it coming right up" Zeffirelli was more than I could bear.

Charles Taylor
Modern Review *(1994)*

Robert Zemeckis

Death Becomes Her (1992)—*Death* is Zemeckis's attempt at an adult film (adult in the sense of it being aimed over the heads of thirteen-year-olds).

Graham Linehan
Select *magazine*

3
TELEVISION
AND RADIO

Tv—a clever contradiction derived from the words "Terrible Vaudeville." However, it is our latest medium—we call it a medium because nothing's well done. It has already revolutionized social grace by cutting down parlor conversation to two sentences: "What's on television?" and "Good night!"

Goodman Ace, letter to
Groucho Marx

Life doesn't imitate art. It imitates bad television.

Woody Allen

There's no way anybody's going to take you seriously if you're on a TV show.

Shaun Cassidy

I don't like television, it's for dedicated nonthinkers.

Billy Connolly (1989)

From talk radio to insult radio wasn't really that much of a leap.

Leonore Fleischer
The Fisher King *(1991)*

The only way to get any feeling from a television set is to touch it when you're wet.

Larry Gelbart (1987)

Television is the box they buried entertainment in.

Bob Hope (1985)

There are film buffs and opera buffs, but there is no such thing as a telly buff. Nor should there be, because only the retarded and TV critics should pay so much attention to such an ephemeral, transitory medium.

Victor Lewis-Smith
London Evening Standard

America is the only country in the world that's still in the business of making bombs that can end the world and TV shows that make it seem like a good idea.

Bill Maher
"Politically Incorrect" (1993)

Everybody watches television. But no one really likes it.
Mark C. Miller

What worries me about television is that it takes our minds off our minds.
Robert Orben

On "Murphy Brown" (1992)—It doesn't help . . . when prime time TV has a character . . . bearing a child alone . . . just another lifestyle choice.

Dan Quayle

The polemics of right-wing radio are putting nothing less than hate onto the airwaves, into the marketplace, electing it to office, teaching it in schools, and exalting it as freedom.

Patricia J. Williams
Hate Radio *(1994)*

Television is bubble gum for the mind.

Frank Lloyd Wright

[*This has also been recorded as:* "Television is bubble gum for the eyes."]

NETWORKS

CBS is now owned by a company that makes freezers.
NBC is owned by a company that makes freezers.
ABC is owned by Disney, whose founder is in a freezer.

Paul Reiser, at the Emmy
Awards Ceremony (1996)

British Broadcasting Corp. [BBC]

The BBC does itself untold harm by its excessive
sensitivity. At the first breath of criticism the
Corporation adopts a posture of a hedgehog at bay.

The Annan Committee Report
(1977)

Canadian Broadcasting Co.

The traffic lights at the CBC are forever amber.

Fletcher Markle
Toronto Life *(1978)*

Fox-TV

The network that gave us 100 percent, FDA-approved
crap.

Peter Ko (1997)

The names might change from time to time on Fox—
"Married: With Children," "Herman's Head,"
"Babes," "Down the Shore"—but the formula never
did. Take a sitcom, throw in a couple of women with
large breasts, add a laugh track where the studio
audience whoops and hollers no matter how trite the
material, and run some yahoo promotion touting the
show as "another outrageous comedy from Fox!" For
variety, throw in some bubblegummy teenage angst
programming like "Beverly Hills 90210" or "The
Heights," and you've got yourself a network that Ed
O'Neill himself is proud to appear on.

Philip Michaels (1997)

Fox, the network that seems to be setting out to prove
that it really doesn't belong with the big boys, ten
years after Fox launched its attempt to be the Fourth
Network, sort of the television equivalent of applying
to be the night manager at the Dairy Queen.

Jason Snell (1997)

National Broadcasting Co. (NBC)
NBC = Nasty Broadcasting Co.

Tom Shales
Washington Post *(1997)*

Public Broadcasting Service (PBS)
PBS = Paid for by Bored Spectators.

Anonymous

Public Service Television is for the humor-impaired.

Alan Goldberg
Washington Journalism
Review *(1983)*

The idea of PBS—heavy-duty "Masterpiece Theater,"
Bill Moyers—I hate all that.

Camille Paglia
Hollywood *(1994)*

WB Network
The "We Blow!" network has suddenly brought us,
purely by accident, a show based on a movie starring
Luke Perry.

Jason Snell (1997)

EXECUTIVES

Anonymous TV Executive Producer
"Pauly" (1997)—This was, without a doubt, one of the worst series ever made. . . . The executive responsible—this scar on the face of humanity—should have his Screen Actors' Guild card torn up in front of him. No, he should be given a hundred paper cuts with the card. Then we'll toss him in a swimming pool filled with lemon juice. Then we tear up the card. And burn it. And shoot it into orbit.

The Vidiots

Roone Arledge, chair of ABC-TV
On ABC's extensive sports coverage—Roone Arledge is the executive producer of more games he never saw.

Don Ohlmeyer (of NBC)

The P. T. Barnum of TV news.

Tom Shales
Washington Post *(1997)*

Don Hewitt, executive producer of "60 Minutes"
Looking at "60 Minutes" has roughly the same impact on Hewitt that standing at the edge of an unruffled pool had on Narcissus.

E. J. Kahn
New Yorker *(1982)*

Marta Kauffmann, David Crane, and Kevin Bright, cocreators of "Dream On," "Friends," and "Veronica's Closet"

They are the perfect sitcom producers for NBC since they have no taste and no shame. They'll stoop to anything faster than you can say—well, faster than you can say "faster than you can say."

> *Tom Shales*
> Washington Post *(1997)*

Warren Littlefield, NBC Entertainment president

You have to understand something about Warren. He's a cockroach. He's going to survive nuclear war.

> *Brandon Tartikoff (1996)*

William S. Paley, president of CBS (1901–90)

He looks like a man who has just swallowed an entire human being.

> *Truman Capote*

Aaron Spelling, producer of "Dynasty," "Fantasy Island," and "Beverly Hills 90210"

Tv's most shameless slinger of schlock.

> *Tom Shales*
> Washington Post *(1997)*

Ted Turner, owner of TBS

On Turner's attempts to colorize Citizen Kane—Don't let Ted Turner deface my movie with his crayons.

> *Orson Welles*

NEWSCASTERS

Another lazy breed like actors. These are likewise too lazy to read through their material before delivering it and constantly misemphasize it, pause in the wrong place, etc.

> *Kingsley Amis*
> The Spectator *(1988)*

On the news two dozen events of fantastically different importance are announced in exactly the same tone of voice. The voice doesn't discriminate between a divorce, a horse race, a war in the Middle East.

> *Doris Lessing*

"20/20" is the trashiest stab at candy-cane journalism yet.

> Washington Post *(1978)*

Walter Cronkite (b 1916)
You can learn more by watching "Let's Make a Deal" than you can by watching Walter Cronkite for a month.

> *Monty Hall*

Sam Donaldson (b 1934)
On her cohost at "Prime Time"—A sonata for harp and jackhammer.

> *Diane Sawyer (1989)*

Television's sultan of splutter.

Hugh Sidey (1985)

Bryant Gumbel (b 1948)
Bryant Gumbel is thrilled about his new CBS deal and can't wait to get started alienating the staff of an entirely new network.

Craig Kilborn
"The Daily Show" (1997)

CBS is having a hard time coming up with a name for his new show. Why? Is "Pretentious Jerk" already taken?

Jim Mullen
Entertainment Weekly *(1997)*

Charles Kuralt
He looked like a factory foreman running behind in stock.

Peggy Noonan
What I Saw at the
Revolution *(1990)*

Jane Pauley
Jane will never be the 6:30 anchor. Not strong enough for the time period. Those are still male jobs, like morning radio hosts.

Larry King (1990)

Dan Rather (b 1931)

Now he is a statesman, when what he really wants is
to be what most reporters are, adult delinquents.

> *Peggy Noonan*
> What I Saw at the
> Revolution *(1990)*

Andy Rooney (b 1920)

As a result of the Dr. Kevorkian interview, Andy
Rooney will be getting more airtime on "60
Minutes," which is strange. I thought Kevorkian was
supposed to relieve suffering.

> *Conan O'Brien*
> *"Late Night" (1996)*

SPORTSCASTERS

To get a job you've either got to be pretty or be a big
star or both. Heck, any guy who can string two
sentences together and look good at the same time can
be a sportscaster.

> *Jim Bouton*

There are two professions that one can be hired at
with little experience. One is prostitution. The other
is sportscasting. Too frequently, they become the same.

> *Howard Cosell*

A color commentator is a guy who's paid to talk while everyone goes to the bathroom.

Bill Curry (1968)

Sports announcers are as colorless as a glass of gin. Most of them are like barbers cutting each others' hair. . . . The broken-down ballplayers are the worst, but almost all are equally appalling.

Bill Curry

We're beginning to understand the sportscaster. For example, when one of his favorite teams loses—that's an upset.

Edward Stevenson

Hubie Brown, basketball announcer
Hubie was to network ratings what the *Titanic* was to the winter cruise business.

Pat Williams

Howard Cosell, sports announcer
Sometimes Howard makes me wish I was a dog and he was a fireplug.

Muhammad Ali

A voice that had all the resonance of a clogged Dristan bottle.

Encyclopaedia Britannica
Year Book (1973)

In one year I traveled 450,000 miles by air. That's about eighteen and a half times around the world, or once around Howard Cosell's head.

Jackie Stewart

Joe Garagiola, baseball analyst

Joe Garagiola is considered a humorist, like Mark Twain, who also came from Missouri. The resemblance is purely residential.

Jim Brosnan

Tim McCarver, baseball analyst

McCarver is the preeminent overanalyst of his day. Ask him what time it is, and he'll tell you how a watch works. He can do twenty minutes on the height of infield grass.

Norman Chad
Sports Illustrated *(1992)*

Isiah Thomas, basketball analyst

Since light travels faster than sound, some people appear to be bright until you hear them speak.

Brian Williams (1998)

Dick Vitale, basketball commentator

His voice could peel the skin off a potato.

Norman Chad
Washington Post

Dick Young, sportswriter

A juvenile delinquent who grew up to become a
senior cynic.

Joe Trimble

TALK-SHOW HOSTS

On talk shows—Television emphasizes the deviant so
that it becomes normal. . . . It's become more and
more difficult for people to know the difference
between fame and infamy.

Vicki Abt (1994)

Adipose Talk-Show Host of the Year: Rosie
O'Donnell by a brownie over Ricki Lake, Oprah
Winfrey, and the increasingly corpulent Jenny Jones.

Peter Ko (1997)

Rona Barrett (b 1936)

She has made Hollywood poop marketable on national
TV. . . . She has all the warmth of a self-service station
at 2 A.M.

Tom Shales
Washington Post *(1981)*

Johnny Carson (b 1925)

I can't be on none of these TV chat shows, 'cause
I'd have to say to Johnny Carson, "You're a sad
motherf***er." That's the only way I could put it.

Miles Davis

A chatterbox-equipped night-light.

Terry Galanoy (1972)

It has always been my personal conviction that Carson
is the most overrated amateur since Evelyn and her
magic violin.

Rex Reed

Kathy Lee Gifford (b 1953)

On the news of her husband Frank's alleged affair—When
Kathy Lee first heard about this she was speechless. So
at least something good has come out of it.

*Jay Leno
"The Tonight Show" (1997)*

Larry King (b 1933)

Appearing on "Larry King Live"—Do you mind if I sit
back a little? Because your breath is very bad.

Donald Trump

Rush Limbaugh (b 1951)
Most of us here in the media are what I call
infotainers. . . . Rush Limbaugh is what I call a
disinfotainer. He entertains by spreading
disinformation.

Al Franken (1994)

Do you ever wake up in the middle of the night and
think: "I'm full of hot gas"?

David Letterman
"The Late Show" (1993)

Joan Lunden (b 1950)
She'll be saying goodbye to "Good Morning
America." It's been twenty years, or 884 new-and-
easy-ways-to-cook-chicken segments.

Jim Mullen
Entertainment Weekly *(1997)*

Bob Newhart (b 1929)
M. C. Stammer.

Bruce Fretts
Entertainment Weekly *(1997)*

Geraldo Rivera (b 1943)
If Geraldo Rivera is the first journalist in space, NASA
can test weightlessness on weightlessness.

Anonymous

Roseanne (b 1952)
She's getting her own talk show. Disappointing news
for those who hoped she'd become a mime.

> *Jim Mullen*
> Entertainment Weekly *(1997)*

Barbara Walters (b 1931)
Barbara Walters—manicurist, pedicurist, guru of
kitsch, yenta, maven, gadfly, blabbermouth, and
Mother Confessor to the world.

> *Tom Shales*
> Washington Post *(1980)*

She is said to sleep standing up so the silicone won't
move.

> *"Taki"*
> The Spectator

Oprah Winfrey (b 1954)
The Oprah-trained demand . . . a psychic striptease.

> *Charles Krauthammer*
> U.S. News & World Report
> *(1992)*

Oprah Winfrey and Phil Donahue (b 1935)
Methinks it's safer to allow infected people from India
to enter Britain than to expose ourselves to American
television stars such as these two nincompoops.

> *"Taki"*
> The Times *of London*

4
THEATER

If there's a spirit world, why don't the ghosts of dead artists get together and inhibit bad playwrights from tormenting first-nighters?

Gertrude Atherton
Black Oxen *(1923)*

Stage musicals are gaily irrational to the point of lunacy.

Noël Coward

I find writing about the Canadian theater or drama depressingly like discussing the art of dinghy-sailing among Bedouins.

Merrill Denison

Anonymous Plays and Playwrights

The Cupboard—Bare.

Clive Barnes

Burrito Square—During the overture you hoped it would be good. During the first number you hoped it would be good. After that you just hoped it would be over.

Walter Kerr

Ilya Darling—I think they have made a mistake. They've left the show in Detroit, or wherever it was last warming up, and brought in the publicity stills.

Walter Kerr (1967)

The Red Rainbow—The "Red," I believe, stood for Communism. The "Rainbow" stood for the light in the heavens on the day Communism took over. The audience stood for more than could possibly be imagined.

Walter Kerr

Sing Till Tomorrow—It had two strikes against it. One was the fact you couldn't hear half of it. The other was the half you could hear.

Walter Kerr

Anonymous play—The plot was designed in a light vein that somehow went varicose.

David Lardner

Carrie *performed by The Royal Shakespeare Company* (1988)—Nothing can hide the gala kitsch of a gimmicky, flashy, and ultimately empty show, set somewhere between *Grease* and a nightmare by Norman Rockwell.

Sheridan Morley

Anonymous play—If you don't knit, bring a book.

Dorothy Parker
Vanity Fair

Anonymous play *starring Earl Carroll*—I saw it at a disadvantage—the curtain was up.

Arthur Wimperis

Anonymous play—The audience strummed their catarrhs.

Alexander Woollcott

Marilyn Abrams and Bruce Jordan
Shear Madness (1982)—Sheer Badness.

Anonymous

Shear Madness (1982)—Madness falls a cut below its promise.

Howard Reich
Chicago Tribune

Edward Albee (b 1928)
Tiny Alice (1965)—Edward Albee has called his new play "a mystery story," a description which equally applies as well to its content.

> *Robert Brustein*
> The New Republic

Who's Afraid of Virginia Woolf? (1962)—The pessimism and rage are immature. Immaturity coupled with a commanding deftness is dangerous.

> *Harold Clurman*
> The Nation

Three Tall Women (1995)—It's a play that after you've been there for a short while, you wonder how long this is going to take.

> *Garrison Keillor*
> New York *magazine*

Jeffrey Archer (b 1940)
Beyond All Reasonable Doubt (1987)—Mr. Archer's play seems to have been not so much written as assembled from spare parts.

> *Sheridan Morley*

Samuel Beckett (1906–89)
Waiting for Godot (1960)—It is pretentious gibberish,
without any claim to importance whatsoever. It is
nothing but phony surrealism with occasional
references to Christ and mankind. It has no form, no
basic philosophy, and absolutely no lucidity. It's too
conscious to be written off as mad. It's just a waste of
everybody's time and it made me ashamed to think
that such balls could be taken seriously for a moment.

Noël Coward

Try as I have been since *Waiting for Godot* in the late
'50s, I cannot find in Mr. Beckett's work anything that
remotely qualifies him to be a playwright, let alone a
respected one. . . . There are times when I suspect that
Beckett is a confidence trick perpetrated by a theater-
hating God. He is surely the naked emperor.

Sheridan Morley (1973)

His symbols are seldom more demanding than a
nursery version of *Pilgrim's Progress.* If occasionally we
get them wrong or do not get them at all, we can
safely assume they were not worth deciphering.

Milton Shulman (1955)

Bertolt Brecht (1898–1956)
"The Days of the Commune" (1977)—It has the depth
of a cracker motto, the drama of a dial-a-recipe
service, and the eloquence of a conversation between a
speak-your-weight machine and a whoopee cushion.

Bernard Levin
The Times *of London*

Broadway, New York
Broadway is a branch of the narcotics world run by
actors.

Bertolt Brecht

At the turn of the century, exiles from Middle
America came to Broadway to find their dreams; these
days, Broadway—and New York City—is a nightmare
you're lucky to escape from.

Julie Burchill
The Times *of London (1992)*

As far as Broadway is concerned, a star that is no
longer in the ascendant is already extinct.

Walter Winchell

The hardened artery.

Walter Winchell

Erskine Caldwell (1903–87)

Tobacco Road (1932)—It isn't the sort of entertainment folks buy in the theater, nor ever have bought within my memory.

Burns Mantle
New York Daily News

Mary Chase

Harvey (1970)—An unassuming little comedy that occasionally tickles you, but more often makes you feel itchy.

John Simon

Anton Chekhov (1860–1904)

The Seagull (1896)—What with the strain of trying to follow the cockeyed goings-on of characters called Zarietchnatya and Medvienko . . . my suffering had been intense.

P. G. Wodehouse
Jeeves in the Offing *(1960)*

Comden & Green and Strouse & Adams

Applause! (1970)—Should be called *Clap!*

Los Angeles Times

Noël Coward (1899–1973)

This Was a Man—The first night in New York was fashionable to a degree. Everybody who was anybody was there—that is, they were there till the end of the second act.

Noël Coward

Could I write as witty
As Noël Coward
By my self-esteem
I should be devoward.

> *Ogden Nash*
> New Yorker *(1931)*

John Drinkwater

Abraham Lincoln—This play holds the season's record, thus far, with a run of four evening performances and one matinee. By an odd coincidence, it ran just five performances too many.

> *Dorothy Parker*
> New Yorker *(1927)*

T. S. Eliot (1888–1965)

The Elder Statesman (1958)—A zombie play designed for the living dead. . . . It is a play in which Mr. Eliot mistakes snobbery for ethics, melodrama for tragedy, vulgarity for wit, obscurity for poetry, and sermonizing for philosophy.

> *Alan Brien*
> The Spectator

The Cocktail Party (1950)—The critic in me is alarmed
that a play so deplorably weak in playcraft should be
hailed as something like a masterpiece. The critic in
me is despondent when willful obscurity is greeted as
subtlety, when affected persiflage passes for wit, when
plain flat prose cut into lines of arbitrary length is
loosely given the name of poetry.

> *Alan Dent*
> News Chronicle

Jules Feiffer

Knock Knock (1976)—When my time comes, I expect
to go straight into heaven, no questions asked. I've
earned it by seeing Jules Feiffer's poor play *Knock
Knock* three times.

> *Stanley Kauffmann*
> The New Republic

Grownups (1982)—When it isn't boring, which it is
much of the time, it's repellent.

> *Stanley Kauffmann*
> Saturday Review

George Gershwin (1898–1937)

An American in Paris—It is nauseous claptrap, so dull,
patchy, thin, vulgar, long-winded, and inane that the
average movie audience would be bored by it. This
cheap and silly affair seemed pitifully futile and inept.

> *Herbert F. Peyser*
> New York Telegram *(1928)*

An occasional work of his on a program is all very well, but an entire evening is too much. It is like a meal of chocolate eclairs.

Richard D. Saunders
The Musical Courier *(1937)*

Andre Gregory
Alice in Wonderland *adapted from Lewis Carroll* (1970)—The play, performed by something that aptly calls itself "The Manhattan Project," is a bomb.

John Simon

David Hare (b 1947)
The Secret Rapture (1989)—A pallid imitation of life.

New York Times

Lorenz M. Hart (1895–1943)
A partner, a best friend, and a source of permanent irritation.

Richard Rodgers

Lillian Hellman (1907–84)
The Little Foxes—The first night is as grisly as an undertaker's picnic, and may be grislier.

Robert Cushman (1982)

George S. Kaufman (1889–1961)
He was a morning glory climbing a pole.

> *Attributed to Alexander*
> *Woollcott*

(Sir) Andrew Lloyd Webber (b 1948)
Sunset Boulevard (1993)—What was that great line of Gloria Swanson's in the film when William Holden tells her she used to be big? "I'm still big; it's the pictures that got small." Now it's the ticket prices which are still big—and the shows which got small.

> *Julie Burchill*

Evita (1978)—The composer has been particularly applauded for the eclecticism of its idiom, as if drawing on six varieties of rubbish was more praiseworthy, or for that matter, more difficult, than employing one. . . . It may not only be the worst night I ever spent in the theater but the worst evening anywhere.

> *Bernard Levin*
> The Times *of London*

Sunset Boulevard (1993)—It is an old joke to say you come out of a show humming the scenery, but this is the first time I have encountered a staircase you could set to music.

> London Today

Lloyd Webber is a bleedin' cowboy—he's terrible, absolutely terrible. I don't know how he's ever got anything published, let alone on stage. . . . People like that shouldn't be allowed out.

Kirsty MacColl (1989)

Jesus Christ Superstar (1970)—The success of a show like this, technically brilliant and editorially mindless, suggests that it is possible to put together a musical with all the soul of a Boeing 747 and roughly the same sense of style.

Sheridan Morley (1972)

Phantom of the Opera (1986)—Impoverished of artistic personality and passion.

Frank Rich
New York Times *(1988)*

Whistle Down the Wind (1997)—A complete miss.

Lloyd Rose
Washington Post

Starlight Express—Not even worth a low commotion.

Ian Shuttleworth
London City Limits *(1992)*

Sunset Boulevard (1993)—A stepchild to the [Billy Wilder] movie.

USA Today

Sunset Boulevard (1993)—I have come away from Sunset Boulevard with the impression that Sir Andrew has reacted to the charges of musical plagiarism by stealing from his own music.

> Wall Street Journal

Lloyd Webber's music is everywhere, but so is AIDS.

> *Malcolm Williamson (1992)*

Frank Loesser (1910–69) and Abe Burrows (1910–85)

Guys and Dolls (1953)—An interminable, and overwhelming, and in the end, intolerable bore.

> *Harold Hobson*
> The Times *of London*

Joshua Logan (1908–88)

The Wisteria Tree, *Logan's adaptation of Chekhov's* The Cherry Orchard *set in the American South*—Southern-fried Chekhov.

> *Anonymous cast member*

David Mamet (b 1947)

The American Buffalo (1977)—The play just marks time with dumb, nasty, mildly funny verbalizations and petty gripes or flare-ups; gradually, it retreats deeper and deeper under the cover of a sheltering affectlessness.

> *John Simon*
> The Hudson Review

Speed-the-Plow (1988)—Director Jon Best and his trio of American actors are all at sea in the woolly, quasi-existential verbiage of the inscrutable (and insufferable) midsection. . . . To make matters worse, the cast speak their lines as if reciting the Holy Gospel.

Neil Smith (1992)

Arthur Miller (b 1915)

The American Clock (1981)—*The American Clock* leaves Miller essentially where he was . . . a "great" American playwright whose work is mostly mediocre.

Stanley Kauffmann
Saturday Review

Molière (1622–73)

Molière was a smart French plagiarist who hired three guys to do his thinking for him.

D. W. Griffith (1921)

The Misanthrope *performed by the APA-Phoenix Repertory Co.* (1968)—The APA production is as bad as . . . as . . . it is hard to find an adequately monstrous simile. As bad—let me try—as its review by Clive Barnes, who had high praise for this production. . . . Mr. Barnes urges us not only to buy a ticket but to give the company a donation as well. If the money is to be used as an instant retirement fund, I shall be glad to contribute.

John Simon

Anthony Newley (b 1931)
The Good Old Bad Old Days (1973)—It manages momentarily to rise above being *Oh What A Lovely Bore.*

> *Sheridan Morley*

Anne Nichols
Abie's Irish Rose—In its second year, God forbid.

> *Robert Benchley*
> Life

Joyce Carol Oates
Sunday Dinner (1970)—The play is an equation with too many X's for me to figure out any of the whys.

> *John Simon*

Clifford Odets (1906–63)
In the drama of the shrillest hornblower of them all is Clifford Odets. Mr. Odets is certainly determined not to let die the legend that he is the White Hope of the American theater. Not even living in Hollywood and receiving the shekels of the mammon of movies has daunted his faith in himself. And by blowing his horn enough, he has convinced a few otherwise sensible critics that the Hope has become a reality.

> *Grenville Vernon*

Eugene O'Neill (1888–1953)
Strange Interlude (1928)—It will probably interest a
comparatively small public. It is solid gray in tone,
slow-paced and repetitious in performance, and
forbidding in length.

> *Burns Mantle*
> New York Daily News

Joe Orton (1933–67)
Loot (1968)—*Loot* makes the impression of having been
written without any feeling at all; it seems disengaged
even from the objects of its scorn. Orton's coldness
leaves me cold.

> *Harold Clurman*
> The Nation

What the Butler Saw (1970)—When people laugh at Joe
Orton's comedies, as indeed some of them sometimes
do, I wonder if they aren't doing exactly what Mr.
Orton wished them to do. There was something in
the late Mr. Orton that hungered to kill comedy. . . .
It is no laughing matter, unless we are willing to laugh
at the old jokes after the heart of them has been
deliberately carved out.

> *Walter Kerr*
> The Times *of London*

Prick Up Your Ears—No thanks!

> The Spectator

John Osborne (1929–94)

Look Back in Anger (1956)—It sets up a wailing wall for the postwar generation of under-thirties. It aims at being a despairing cry but achieves only the stature of a self-pitying snivel.

> *Milton Shulman*
> London Evening Standard

Look Back in Anger (1956)—Mr. Osborne will have other plays in him, and perhaps he will settle down, now that he has got this off his mind.

> *J. C. Trewin*
> Illustrated London News

Harold Pinter (b 1930)

The Birthday Party (1958)— . . . like a vintage Hitchcock thriller which has, in the immortal tearstained words of Orson Welles, been "edited by a cross-eyed studio janitor with a lawn mower."

> *Alan Brien*
> The Spectator

Betrayal (1978)—A very insubstantial so-what piece of work. . . . The play is, to say the least, a far from stimulating experience.

> *Clive Hirschorn*

The Homecoming (1965)—Long stretches of the second act seem to be no more than the actions of a tired man keeping the ball in the air; the positive motivelessness becomes negatively aimless and shallow; he seems to be imitating his own style, asking himself what Pinter would do now, and then doing it.

Bernard Levin

David Rabe
Streamers (1976)—The American theater may be short on lots of things, but one gift it's loaded with—the ability to make mountains out of molehills. A current playwrighting molehill is David Rabe.

Stanley Kauffmann
The New Republic

Richard Rodgers (1902–79) and
Oscar Hammerstein II (1895–1961)
Carousel (1945)—"You'll Never Walk Alone," which has always seemed to me an embarrassment, is the show's one resounding dud. Or am I alone?

John Gross
London Telegraph *(1992)*

The Royal Court, London
Lots of plays at the Royal Court are about people who talk away for hours and still can't communicate with each other, and become more and more wretched.

Noël Coward

Anthony Shaffer

Sleuth (1970)—To the question just what does the
expression "too clever by half" mean? Anthony
Shaffer's *Sleuth* will serve as an answer. . . . The
number of plot reversals would make a shuttle pale
with envy. . . . His style is sheer chinoiserie, piling
lacquered screens of paradox upon pagodas of
hyperbole.

John Simon

William Shakespeare (1564–1616)

Hamlet—The goddamnest bore in literature, that
pompous ass the ghost.

John Barrymore

I am more easily bored with Shakespeare and have
suffered more ghastly evenings with Shakespeare than
with any other dramatist I know.

Peter Brook

Taming of the Shrew—A play so loutish in its humor,
and so lacking in appeal to the mind, that Hollywood
naturally made it first choice when the filming of
Shakespeare began.

Ivor Brown

There is an upstart crow beautified with feathers. That with his tyger's heart wrapt in a player's hide, supposes[2] he is as well able to bombast out a blank verse as the best of you; and being an absolute Johannes Factotum, is, in his own conceit, the only Shakescene in a country.

Robert Greene (1590)

Macbeth *performed by the English Shakespeare Company* (1992)—Thanes ain't what they used to be.

Kenneth Hurren

Cymbeline—I hesitate to waste criticism on unresisting imbecility.

Samuel Johnson

Othello *directed by Franco Zeffirelli* (1961)—For the eye, too much; for the ear, too little; for the mind, nothing at all.

Bernard Levin

Macbeth—Prompter Steals the Show in UCLA Macbeth.

Los Angeles Times
headline (1919)

Twelfth Night (1663)—After dinner to the Duke's house, and there we saw *Twelfth Night* acted well, though it be but a silly play, and not related at all to the name of the day.

Samuel Pepys
Diary

George Bernard Shaw (1856–1950)
Mrs. Warren's Profession (1905)—The limit of stage decency was reached last night in one of Mr. Shaw's "unpleasant comedies." . . . If New York's sense of shame is not aroused to hot indignation at this theatrical insult, it is indeed a sad plight. . . . The only way to expurgate *Mrs. Warren's Profession* is to cut the whole play out. You cannot have a clean pig stye. The play is an insult to decency. . . . And, worst of all, it countenances the most revolting form of degeneracy.

Nym Crinkle
New York Herald

I remember coming across him at the Grand Canyon and finding him peevish, refusing to admire it or even look at it properly. He was jealous.

J. B. Priestley

Concerning no subject would Shaw be deterred by the minor accident of total ignorance from penning a definitive opinion.

Roger Scruton

It is disappointing to report that George Bernard Shaw appearing as George Bernard Shaw is sadly miscast in the part. Satirists should be heard and not seen.

Robert Sherwood

The way Bernard Shaw believes in himself is very refreshing in these atheistic days, when so many people believe in no God at all.

Israel Zangwill

R. C. Sherriff (1896–1975)
Journey's End (1942)—There are times in his play when, judging from the comportment of his soldiers in their dugout, one can't be sure whether what is going on outside is a war or a Pinero rehearsal.

George Jean Nathan

Neil Simon (b 1927)
Jake's Women (1992)—A crushingly vacuous play. The writing is slick and dreary, full of those amiable New York wisecracks that can yawn so wide between theater and reality.

John Peter
The Times *of London*

Last of the Red Hot Lovers (1969)—According to a famous schoolboy boner, Shakespeare wrote tragedies, comedies, and errors. Neil Simon has yet to write a tragedy, but his comedies and errors are legion.

John Simon

Stephen Sondheim (b 1930)

How could you compare Stephen Sondheim to God? At least God knows how to compose a melody.

Anonymous letter in New York *magazine (1994)*

Into the Woods (1986)—After Sondheim's *Into the Woods,* I have resolved not to go to another musical unless supplied with a written affidavit that it contains at least three hummable tunes.

Philip Norman

Joseph Stein, Jerry Bock, and Sheldon Harnick

Fiddler on the Roof (1964)—Musical? Schmusical!

Irving Berlin (1964)

Tom Stoppard (b 1937)

Rosencrantz and Guildenstern Are Dead (1967)—It is the kind of play that one might enjoy more at a second hearing, if only the first time through hadn't left such a strong feeling that once is enough.

London Telegraph

Brandon Thomas (1856–1914)
Charley's Aunt—J. R. Crawford directed rehearsals
with all the airy deftness of a rheumatic deacon
producing *Macbeth* for a church social.

Noël Coward

Leo Tolstoy (1828–1910)
Redemption—It is not what you might call sunny.
I went into the Plymouth Theater a comparatively
young woman, and I staggered out of it three hours
later, twenty years older, haggard and broken with
suffering.

Dorothy Parker
Vanity Fair *(1928)*

Kenneth Tynan (1927–80)
Oh, Calcutta! (1969)—It is a mistake to promise more
than you can perform in sex and even more in
comedy.

Anonymous

Oh, Calcutta! (1969)—Its game is basically the sort of
exhibition of sexual voyeurism that used to be
available to the frustrated and the mentally warped in
the side-turnings of a certain kind of seaport.

Ronald Butt

Oscar Wilde (1854–1900)
Lady Windermere's Fan (1892)—My dear Sir, I have
read your manuscript. Oh, my dear Sir.

> *Anonymous rejection letter*
> *(1892)*

A fatuous cad.

> *Henry James*

Wilde and his epigrams are shown up as brilliant bores
Before the unpretentious penetration of the comment
     that—
It never rains but it pours.

> *Ogden Nash*
> I'll Take the Bromide, Please
> *(1940)*

Tennessee Williams (1911–83)
On the filmed version of Orpheus Descending—Darling,
they've absolutely ruined your perfectly dreadful play.

> *Tallulah Bankhead*

After seeing his plays, one is left feeling that Williams
is basically a sentimentalist who fluctuates like a
thermometer, in uncertain weather, between bathos
and poetic rhetoric.

> *Signi Falf*
> Modern Drama *(1958)*

Vieux Carré—The characters march on, one-two-three-four, like automata on a Swiss clock, each bearing the scars of use in earlier Williams plays.

> *Michael Feingold*
> Village Voice *(1977)*

Tennessee Williams often writes like an arrested adolescent who disarmingly imagines that he will attain stature if (as young boys are advised in Dixie) he loads enough manure in his shoes.

> Time

Lanford Wilson

A Tale Told (1981)—If there was a Nobel Prize for Sincere Imitation, Lanford Wilson would be a leading contender in the drama department. . . . Wilson has merely taken an extremely tired diluted-Ibsen ploy . . . and has run it through his typewriter yet again. Sincerely, *A Tale Told* could be called *A Form Filled.*

> *Stanley Kauffmann*
> Saturday Review

5
MUSIC

Roy Acuff (1903–93)

To hell with Roosevelt! To hell with Babe Ruth! To hell with Roy Acuff!

Japanese soldiers'
war cry (1945)

Bryan Adams (b 1959)

"I'm Ready"—Another opus to self-abuse from the horrible MTV "Unplugged" series. A man to whom half-light will always be a friend, Bryan Adams boldy uses the exact same formula as "Everything I Do."

Jane Bussmann
London Guardian *(1998)*

"Live! Live! Live!"—Awful! Awful! Awful! What is it with Canadians and rock music? When they're good, they are very very good. When they're bad, they are Bryan Adams. A terrifyingly expert purveyor of banality who tramples out potent but characterless rock ordinaire.

Charles Shaar Murray (1994)

Victoria Adams ("Posh" of the Spice Girls)

Posh Spice is not posh at all but is in fact Relatively Common Spice.

Arena *(1998)*

America

"A Horse with No Name"—You're in the desert. You've got nothing to do. Name the freaking horse!

Rich Jeni

Louis Armstrong (1898–1971)

The most famous jazz musician of them all was a tubby old trumpet player who ended up singing "Hello Dolly!" with Streisand while wiping his forehead with a soggy handkerchief like some lard-butt umpire at Wrigley Field on nickel beer night.

Spy *(1994)*

Arrested Development

Creates the illusion that such hedonism is doing your bit for the homeless, single mothers, etc. etc.

Melody Maker *(1994)*

The Auteurs
It's all a bit Steely Dan. We fought wars to get rid of that stuff.

Mark E. Smith (1997)

Charles Aznavour (b 1924)
He's so worn by experience he's got bags under his head.

Clive James (1974)

The Beatles
Bad-mannered little shits.

Noël Coward

Musically, this reviewer cannot understand the fervor of the Beatles' admirers. . . . The Beatles are a run-of-the-mill rock 'n' roll attraction.

Nat Hentoff (1964)

Chuck Berry (b 1926)
I love his work, but I couldn't warm to him even if I was cremated next to him.

Keith Richards

The B-52s
"Love Shack" (1990)—It's really irritating and falsely happy.

Victoria Adams
("Posh" of the Spice Girls)
(1997)

Art Blakey (1919–90)
On Blakey's trademark stick-twirling showmanship—Son, the music is on the drums, not in the air.

Chick Webb

Marc Bolan (of T. Rex) (1947–77)
You sure got a funny little voice.

Jimi Hendrix (1967)

Michael Bolton
Come back, Engelbert Humperdinck, all is forgiven!

GQ *(1995)*

"This Is Michael Bolton" (1993)—Third-rate maulings of soul classics from the lionlike pelvic thruster.

London Guardian

Bon Jovi
"Bed of Roses" (1993)—A power ballad so leaden it doubles up as a pencil.

Paul Lester

"Living in Sin" (1989)—A slushy mumbling piece of shit.

Mick Mercer

A simpleton's version of rock 'n' roll.

Adam Sweeting

Jon Bon Jovi (b 1962)

He sounds like he's got a brick dangling from his willy,
and a food mixer making purée of his tonsils.

Paul Lester

Wembley Stadium Concert, London (1988)—
Bon Jovi danced about the stage with all the charisma
of car-park attendants who've watched all the Mick
[Jagger] and Rod [Stewart] videos and practiced hard
in front of their mirrors . . . and still got it wrong.

Steve Sutherland

Bono (of U2) (b 1960)

Bono would love to be six foot tall and thin and
good-looking. But he's not. He reminds me of a
mountain goat.

Ian McCulloch

It's easy to get fooled by Bono. He's a real con
but he shows his colors too often, that's where the
bubble butt blows it. If he played that shit in my
neighborhood, the local crack dealers would have
taken him out a long time ago.

Henry Rollins (1993)

My window cleaner has got more to say than him.

Mark E. Smith (1990)

If you are one of Bono's brain cells, you'll be lonely.

Tom (of the Mekons) (1989)

Pat Boone (b 1934)
If I had a son, I'd like him to be like Pat Boone—till he was three hours old.

Frank Sinatra (1966)

David Bowie (b 1947)
His flamboyant drive for pop-star status has stamped him . . . as a naked opportunist and a poseur.

Ben Gerson
Rolling Stone *(1973)*

Bowie never met a trend he could not exploit.

Greg Kot
Chicago Tribune *(1997)*

On Bowie's 1970s "Ziggy Stardust" phase—It's just rock 'n' roll with lipstick on.

John Lennon

He's just doing what Phil May of the Pretty Things used to do. He's just wearing different clothes.

Van Morrison (1973)

I resent people you grow up admiring who turn out to be the biggest tossers, like David Bowie. I just wish he'd been killed in a car accident after he'd finished "Low."

Robert Smith

Garth Brooks (b 1962)
"We Shall Be Free"—More American lies . . . from the billion-selling man with the hat who always looks like he's just farted.

Ross Fortune (1992)

Meredith Brooks
"Bitch" (1997)—Her grating voice (a computer-generated blend of Alanis and Sheryl). . . . I do not feel ashamed turning the volume down every time.

David Browne
Entertainment Weekly

James Brown (b 1933)
On Brown's prison sentence—Papa's got plenty of brand new mailbags to sew.

Len Brown

Emma Bunton ("Baby" of the Spice Girls)
She has crow's-feet and a bum like an old couch—not very "baby," is it?

Arena *(1998)*

Montserrat Caballé (b 1933)

"Tosca in Tokyo"—featured Montserrat Caballé. The Japanese were impressed. It was clear that they hadn't seen anything that size since the battleship *Missouri* anchored in Tokyo Bay in 1945.

Clive James (1979)

Belinda Carlisle

"Leave a Light On" (1989)—It's kind of like watching a chicken try to fly. You wish it would stop, or turn into a swan, or even just stop trying so hard.

The Stud Brothers

Bob Carlisle

"Butterfly Kisses" (1997)—Carlisle's white-soul groan could make God cringe.

David Browne
Entertainment Weekly

The Carpenters

"Close to You"—Do I really want to be near somebody who causes birds to appear suddenly? Didn't Alfred Hitchcock do a horror movie about this?

Dave Barry
Book of Bad Songs *(1997)*

Enrico Caruso (1873–1921)

"Madame Butterfly" (1907)—Caruso's celebrated singing does not appeal very much more than the barking of a dog in a faraway wood.

Jihei Hashigushi

Richard Clayderman (b 1954)

He is to piano playing as David Soul is to acting; he makes Jacques Loussier sound like Bach; he reminds us how cheap potent music can be.

Richard Williams

Glenn Close

"Sunset Boulevard" (1994)—Glenn Close . . . sings in a girlish, quavering soprano, and when it reaches into the lower register it doesn't dip—it hurls into the abyss, kicking and screaming. There isn't a moment when you think you're watching a human being. (And there isn't a moment in Andrew Lloyd Webber's score when you think you're listening to music.)

Steve Vineberg
Modern Review

Kurt Cobain (of Nirvana) (1967–94)

Kurt Cobain was . . . a worthless shred of human debris.

Rush Limbaugh (1994)

In Memoriam:
So, Farewell then Kurt Cobain,
You shot yourself because you were depressed.
I once listened to one of your records.
So I know how you must have felt.

"E. J. Thribb"
Private Eye *(1994)*

Natalie Cole (b 1950)

"Starting Over" (1989)—If you want to avoid dire
rubbish like this, just look on any records for the
names [of producers] Michael Masser and Narada
Michael Walden. If you see either name or both
names, run.

Ian McCann

Phil Collins (b 1951) and Genesis

Phil could have been John Lennon, but he opted for
Paul McCartney.

Anonymous (1997)

Earl's Court Concert, London (1992)—Games master
Phil Collins and his anonymous chums gave full value
for money as they paraded their treacly, interminable
songs in and out of the fancy hardware. Unfortunately,
atmosphere was not in the air tonight. . . . The aural
Valium disguised as karmic snooze-surround was
apparent. . . . Fair's fair. The virtual reality graphics
were super. Shame about the actual boredom.

> *Max Bell*
> London Evening Standard

Anyone who takes themselves deadly serious is funny,
like Phil Collins, who sounds like an air conditioner.

> *Michael Heath*

"The Way We Walk, Vol. 1" (1992)—The continued
existence of Genesis provides incontestable proof that
there is no God. Featuring, as always, Beelzebub on
drums and vocals.

> *Adam Higginbotham*
> Select

Alice Cooper (b 1948)

Cooper is a master charlatan; indeed, he has elevated
charlatanry to a higher artistic plane than anybody else.

> *Charles Shaar Murray (1974)*

"Bed of Nails" (1989)—Not really as good as "Poison," which wasn't the least bit good. . . . This is a bit like mugging a dosser, it's always unpleasant.

The Stud Brothers

Elvis Costello (b 1955)
Elvis is terrible, all fat and sweaty. Can't dance either.

Ian McCulloch

Kevin Coyne (b 1944)
It's said that he's very big in Germany, which is like saying cricket is popular in Albania.

Angus Deayton (1993)

Crowded House
They are big in Canada, which sums them up really.

David Stubbs

Billy Ray Cyrus (b 1961)
"These Boots Were Made for Walking" (1992)—Well, I know for a fact that it isn't my mum who keeps buying all the Billy Ray Cyrus records.

Nick Coleman

Da Brat
"Anuthatantrum" (1996)—Sounding about as scary as a schoolyard boast.

Entertainment Weekly

Miles Davis (1926–91)

An emaciated junkie who used to play with his back to the audience and occasionally sprayed the folks in the front row while spitting into his instrument.

Spy (1994)

Chris De Burgh (b 1950)

The ugliest man alive. The Valium of the Menopausal Generation.

Barry Egan (1988)

Deep Blue Something

"Breakfast at Tiffany's" (1996)—The best reason to turn the radio off.

Entertainment Weekly

Def Leppard

"Adrenalize" (1992)—There's never even the slightest suggestion that things might even get a little out of hand, that something unexpected or shocking might occur, which is a sad comment on a supposedly wild genre.

Andy Gill

They're the George Bush of rock. They're just pieces of animation, they're faceless, a blur nobody can define.

Jim Steinman (1989)

Zack De La Rocha
(of Rage Against the Machine)
"Evil Empire" (1996)—Screaming that war is bad and corporations are worse. . . . He makes you yearn for the comparative subtleties of Peter, Paul, and Mary.

Rolling Stone

De La Soul
"Buhloone Mind Stage"—De La Soul are indeed dead. Or at least sleeping the kind of sleep that people only wake up from in Stephen King novels.

Melody Maker (1994)

Sandy Dennis
"Falling" (1993)—Teenyboppy disco music for restless schoolgirls.

Ray Douglas

Depeche Mode
Perhaps they should try telling some jokes on their records, it might cheer them up a bit.

Laura Lee Davies (1993)

Neil Diamond (b 1941)
"The Jazz Singer" (1980)—What is jazz to Neil Diamond and what is Neil Diamond to jazz? Old title has nothing to do with music on display here and would seem meaningless to modern audiences.

Variety

The Dick Nixons

"Paint the White House Black" (1992)—We may deserve the government we get, but do we deserve this?

Jeremy Clarke
Select

Bo Diddley (b 1928)

If he ever gets out of the key of E, he might be dangerous.

Jerry Lee Lewis

Celine Dion

"Falling into You" (1996)—A nuance-impaired French-Canadian belting American power ballads with the occasional washed-out reggae twist. This can't be why the term "world music" was invented.

David Browne
Entertainment Weekly

Dire Straits

The dullards of rock.

Time Out *(1992)*

Placido Domingo (b 1941)

"Mozart's Arias" (1992)—A collection of contextless tenor scenes and arias, sung with undoubted passion but comparatively little grace, is simply too monotonous to make for an edifying—or even satisfying—recital.

Ian Brunskill

"Barber of Seville" (1992)—A Figaro who sounds like
an Otello in need of a new navigator; too light,
obviously tenorial in tone, lugubrious in lines which
require verbal agility, utterly devoid of wit.

Hugh Canning
The Times *of London*

[*The same critic later repeated his
view of the performance in* BBC
Music *magazine*—One of the
most humorless characterizations
of the "Barber" on record, and
Domingo sounds like an Otello
who took the wrong turning at
the heel of the Italian
Peninsula.]

"Entre dos Mundos" (1992)—About as embarrassing as
such things manage to be—which is considerable. . . .
If you love the Eurovision Song Contest or Barcelona
Airport's Muzak, you'll love this.

Michael S. Rohan

Duran Duran
"Girls on Film: The Video" (1981)—Repulsive piece
of gang-bang voyeurism.

Dave Hill (1986)

"Big Thing" (1989)—Would I dig this if I was
thirteen? Or would the pervasive image of Simon
le Bon's trouser-minnow be too scary?

Dave Jennings

They're just crap. Shit. Publicly they're assholes. They do immeasurable damage. They damage music by doing what the cavalry did to the Indians . . . massacre it, kill it.

Mike Scott

Bob Dylan (b 1941)
Pat Garrett & Billy the Kid (1973)—The music is so oppressive that when it stops we feel giddy with relief, as if a tooth had suddenly stopped aching.

Vincent Canby
New York Times

Zimmerman? Zimmerframe more like, you useless, cactus-faced crock of cack.

Melody Maker

How is it possible to play the harmonica, professionally, for thirty years and still show no sign of improvement?

David Sinclair (1993)

ECM record label
A massive musical mush-making machine, run by one Manfred Eicher, whose avowed purpose it appears to be to turn us all into blancmange.

Anonymous (1981)

The ECM sound is as bland as a Ford Pinto full of Cream of Wheat.

Anonymous

The music world's equivalent of a cashmere Issey Miyake overcoat.

Stuart Maconie
Q *magazine (1997)*

Edward "Duke" Ellington (1899–1974)
A self-anointed duke who wrote ghastly songs like "Satin Doll."

Spy *(1994)*

Emerson, Lake and Palmer
"Live at the Albert Hall, London" (1992)—If it was Ralph Waldo Emerson, Veronica Lake, and Arnold Palmer, the rest of the world would have to sit up and take notice, but it's Keith, Greg, and Carl, on the run from the taste police in their leather trousers and horrendous embroidered shirts, ready to perpetrate more aesthetic crimes in the name of pomp-rock.

Ben Thompson

En Vogue
Comparing En Vogue to the greats of soul is like comparing the Monkees to the Beatles.

David Sinclair
The Times *of London (1992)*

[Davy Jones preferred a Monkees–Beatles comparison of "General Hospital" to "Star Trek."]

Enya (b 1961)
She makes All About Eve sound like Public Enemy.

Stuart Maconie

A foul, cold-hearted technician whose music is so
sterile that were it possible to bottle it, you could use
it to clean lavatories.

Melody Maker (1992)

Erasure
Music to take back slightly shop-soiled shirts for a
refund to.

David Stubbs (1989)

Gloria Estefan
She sings like she's got Babycham coursing through
her veins rather than blood.

Simon Reynolds (1989)

The Eurythmics
If music be the food of love, why do the Eurythmics
insist on serving up Spam and chips all the time?

Pauline (of Pluto) (1989)

"Revival" (1989)—Ignore the title . . . this simply
repeats their tired prog-rock formula.

Robert Yates

Bryan Ferry (b 1945)

"Girl of My Best Friend"—If you like deeply sexy syrup with the odd vulnerable warble in different guises, then you'll love this.

Emma Perry (1993)

"Let's Stick Together"—This sounds as though it was remixed by Bryan's drunken chauffeur, who happened to be hanging out in the studio one night.

Jonh Wilde

Kirsten Flagstad (1895–1962)

I have heard Toscanini conduct "Falstaff" and Flagstad sing "Isolde"—the only time that I cried at the opera.

A. J. P. Taylor
A Personal History *(1983)*

Julia Fordham

"Woman of the Eighties"—Yuppie Soul! Words can't go far enough to say how abhorrent this muck is. Burn her at the stake! Aretha Franklin for the eighties, designed by a committee.

Ian Gittens

Foreigner

I've seen Bauhaus, so I've seen bad, and I've seen Foreigner, so I've seen worse.

Steve Sutherland

4 Non Blondes

Cozy, cowardly M.O.R. slop from the sort of hags
they used to duck in village ponds.

Melody Maker (1994)

Aretha Franklin (b 1942)

"Check This Out!" (1989)—Unfortunately, Aretha's
"Check This Out!" reminds me of a cop who rather
clumsily insists on shouting "Yo!" whenever a kid
passes by.

Robert Yates

Vince Gill (b 1957)

"High Lonesome Road" (1996)—His voice, a sort of
soupy high tenor, can be insufferably cloying. . . . If
Gill shut up and played the guitar, he'd be a lot poorer,
but the world wouldn't be.

Tony Scherman
Entertainment Weekly

Ian Gillan (of Deep Purple) (b 1945)

He is the most belligerently awful person ever. . . . I
find him a very coarse man, bordering on repulsive.
He's obnoxious when he's drunk, he really is.

Ritchie Blackmore (1991)

The Go-Go's

"Vacation"—Uncool jerkoffs!

Anonymous (1982)

Guns N' Roses
"Slane Castle Concert, Ireland" (1992)—It went downhill from the entrance.

Melody Maker

Arlo Guthrie (b 1947)
In a world nodding and bobbing with boring folk singers, Arlo bores his way to the top.

Gavin Millar
The Listener

Sammy Hagar (b 1947)
Everyone hates Sammy Hagar. Who doesn't?

Parry Gripp
(of Nerf Herder) (1996)

Geri Halliwell
(formerly "Ginger" of the Spice Girls)
The "Madame" of the group. . . . In reality she is just another cult leader ready to throw a Kool-Aid party in a jungle, where they'll board a spaceship and fly off to the home planet of Spice.

Why We Hate the
Spice Girls *(1997)*

Hanson
That Fraternal trio of Aryan boy waifs.

Troy Patterson
Entertainment Weekly *(1998)*

Deborah Harry (of Blondie) (b 1945)

The face that launched a thousand whores.

The Stud Brothers

Sophie B. Hawkins

"Damn, I Wish I Was Your Lover" (1992)—She should get out more.

Melody Maker

Buddy Holly (1936–59)

He has always struck me as the type more likely to be found serving in a hamburger bar or delivering the soft drinks.

Paul Anka

Hootie and the Blowfish

"Fairweather Johnson" (1996)—Hootie and the Blowfish never pretended to be more than a basic hardworking band. "Fairweather Johnson" proves it with a vengeance.

Rolling Stone

Whitney Houston (b 1963)

"I'm Every Woman" (1993)—I'll tell you one woman who you certainly aren't. And that's Chaka Khan. Leave soul songs to the actual human beings they were written for in the first place, Whitney, you walking, smooching, cooing MTV android from designer jean hell!

Mr. Agreeable

Mick Hucknall (of Simply Red) (b 1960)
We talk of the death of soul, and all he wants to do is sing for his supper.

Ian Gittens

Ice-T (b 1958)
Just another black guy looking for his fifteen minutes of fame.

Charlton Heston
Esquire *(1997)*

"Return of the Real" (1996)—Ice has covered this territory so often, he might as well have called this "Regurgitation of the Rote."

Tom Sinclair
Entertainment Weekly

Inxs
"Heaven Sent" (1992)—An appalling, blaring, incoherent, neon nightmare, rather like staring at a searchlight.

Melody Maker

Iron Maiden
An aural effect akin to the sensation of having a car battery dropped on the foot.

Anonymous (1990)

They can't have any idea what they sound like,
otherwise they'd sound like something else.

> *Ian McCann*
> New Musical Express

The Jacksons
"2300 Jackson Street" (1989)—Listening to it feels not
unlike being drowned in sweet sherry.

> *Dave Jennings*

Jermaine Jackson (b 1954)
He has the mental acumen and agility of a hedgehog.
If Michael is a pair of pristine white socks, Jermaine is
the old grubby nylon pair with the big toes sticking
out.

> *Ian Gittens (1989)*

Michael Jackson (b 1958)
Appearing on "Oprah" (1993)—With his womanly
voice, stark white skin and Medusa hair, his gash of
red lipstick, heavy eyeliner, almost nonexistent nose
and lopsided face, Jackson was making this TV
appearance in order to scotch all rumors that he is not
quite normal.

> *Craig Brown*
> The Times *of London*

Lisa-Marie's live-in babysitter.

> GQ *(1995)*

Michael Jackson is not a star. He's got no business being on stage. He's too fat, he wears underwear on the outside, and he's been accused of abusing children.

Nash Kato
(of Urge Overkill) (1993)

Fame has sent a number of celebrities off the deep end, and in the case of Michael Jackson, to the kiddy pool.

Bill Maher
"Politically Incorrect" (1994)

Wembley Stadium Concert, London (1992)—He hasn't just lost the plot, he's lost the whole library!

Melody Maker

"Scream"—Oh, put it away, for goodness sake.

John O'Connell (1995)

"Bad" (1989)—Michael Jackson's album was only called "Bad" because there wasn't enough room on the sleeve for "Pathetic."

Prince

"Blood on the Dance Floor: History in the Mix" (1997)—For several years the pallid one has looked like a ghost of his former self. Now he sounds like one.

Tom Sinclair
Entertainment Weekly

He now looks like a Barbie doll that has been whittled at by a malicious brother.

Thomas Sutcliffe (1993)

As for his body, it gave a whole new meaning to "White Christmas."

TNT *magazine (1996)*

Mick Jagger (b 1943)

I think Mick Jagger would be astounded and amazed if he realized to how many people he is not a sex symbol but a mother image.

David Bowie

On rumors of an affair with Jagger—How could I possibly have a sexual relationship with a fifty-year-old fossil? I have a beautiful boyfriend of twenty-eight . . . why should I swap that for a dinosaur?

Carla Bruni (1992)

He is about as sexy as a pissing toad.

Truman Capote

"Wandering Spirit" (1993)—Wandering spirit indeed. Prevaricating ponce more like.

Nick Coleman

After Jagger explained that the wrinkles on his face were just laugh lines—Surely nothing could be that funny?

> George Melly (1995)
>
> [Chet Baker said a similar thing about himself some years earlier.]

"Sweet Thing" (1993)—A stab at "modern" rock-funk but the beat-and-bass-line creaks, I swear, like an arthritic hip. . . . He's trying to come over like a randy teenager, when he should be into gardening or something. Leave it out, granddad.

> Simon Reynolds

Jagger sounds like his mouth is full of putty.

> Chris Roberts

Jane's Addiction
"Kettle Whistle" (1998)—You either buy into Perry Farrell's "Robert Plant does Fagin" shtick or you don't.

> Steve Mirkin
> Entertainment Weekly

Billy Joel (b 1949)
Bob Dylan is so brilliant. To me, he makes William Shakespeare sound like Billy Joel.

> George Harrison

Perfectly balanced. Chips on both shoulders.

Q magazine (1986)

Elton John (b 1947)
If you mention the Queen to most Australian kids,
they think you mean Elton John.

Kathy Lette

His writing is limited to songs for dead blondes.

Keith Richards

Grace Jones (b 1952)
Today the Ice Queen is a soggy (micro)chip, about as
risqué as a double entendre.

Paul Lester (1989)

Tom Jones (b 1940)
"A Man and a Half" (1972)—The singer proceeded to
work his way through twenty or so numbers, shaking
himself the while like an actor auditioning for St. Vitus.
Baring his teeth like an indignant racehorse, Mr. Jones
mumbled, grunted, and sang his way through one of
the least inspiring star turns it has ever been my duty
to witness.

Sheridan Morley

Journey

A single record like "Louie Louie" by the Kingsmen probably had more influence on the development of rock than Journey's entire output.

Pete Frame

Mark Knopfler (of Dire Straits) (b 1949)

"Money for Nothing"—The singer sounded like he was having a crap as the vocal was being recorded.

Andrew Smith

Lenny Kravitz

"Circus" (1995)—As retro ear candy, "Circus" is strictly snake oil.

Rolling Stone

Leadbelly (Huddie Ledbetter) (1889–1949)

Huddie Ledbetter, frequently known as Leadbelly, had a fairly murky past. I can think of several crimes he committed, including murder twice and influencing Lonnie Donegan.

George Melly
"Jazz Score"

Peggy Lee (b 1920)

The poodle of pomp.

Ross Fortune (1992)

John Lennon (1940–80)

John could be a maneuvering swine, which no one
ever realized.

Paul McCartney

John Lennon and Yoko Ono (b 1933)

Some people exist who like to see their names in print.
John Lennon and Yoko Ono are print junkies.

Germaine Greer
The Listener *(1973)*

We live in a country where John Lennon gets six
bullets in the chest. Yoko Ono's standing right next to
him, not a f***ing bullet. WILL YOU EXPLAIN THAT TO
ME, GOD?

Denis Leary

Liberace (1919–87)

Let's get one thing straight. Liberace is a skilled
artist—but his art is comedy, not music.

Anonymous (1955)

This appalling man, and I use the word appalling in no other way than its true sense of terrifying, . . . reeks of emetic language that can only make grown men long for a quiet corner, an aspidistra, a handkerchief, and the old heave-ho. Without doubt he is the biggest sentimental vomit of all time. Slobbering over his mother, winking at his brother, and counting the cash at every second, this superb piece of calculating candy floss has an answer for every situation.

William Connor
London Daily Mirror *(1956)*
[Liberace sued the newspaper and was awarded £8,000 in damages.]

Liberace is pure art student gone camping.

Peter Freedman
Glad to Be Gray *(1985)*

Living Colour
The Au Pairs of Black Rock.

Simon Reynolds

LV (of Coolio)
He's a narcissistic Barry White. . . . They're a similar shirt size, anyway . . . the Walrus of Self-Love.

Nicholas Barber (1996)

Lyle Lovett (b 1957)

His hair looks like a dead ferret resting on his head.

People

Madonna (b 1958)

Q: What's the difference between Madonna and a
   rottweiler?

A: Lipstick

Bitch *magazine (1993)*

"Erotica"—On the best of days, Madonna has an
average voice. Wearing her heart on her G-string, she
has raided the cupboard for ideas, only to discover that
far more talented artists have beaten her to the cookie
jar.

Mike Cowton (1992)

"Like a Virgin" (1985)—Like hell.

Dave Hill

That ugly, shapeless, toe-sucking slut Madonna. . . .
The difference between Marilyn Monroe and
Madonna is the same difference as exists between
champagne and cat's piss.

John Junor (1992)

Madonna is sleazy. She's an exercise in utter cynicism
and has practically no talent.

Irma Kurtz (1992)

"Erotica" (1992)—What is this, a tribute to Benny Hill or something?

Melody Maker

The high priestess of pop bimbos.

Tony Parsons

She's absolutely crap, and the fact that the only people who buy her records are thirteen- to twenty-year-olds proves that scientifically. You never hear a man say "I listen to Madonna."

Jerry Sadowitz (1989)

Barry Manilow (b 1946)

Barry is bringing out a new range of nose clippers. . . . To the rest of us, they'll be more recognizable as shears.

Angus Deayton (1992)

It was reported that Barry Manilow was taking a year off to write a Broadway musical. . . . Taking a year off from what?

Conan O'Brien
"Late Night" (1996)

Paul McCartney (b 1942)

"Mull of Kintyre"—McCartney should have been prosecuted for his "Mull of Kintyre," which was about as mysterious as the local gas board.

Peter McKay (1992)

He has become the oldest living cute boy in the world.

Anna Quindlen

If I hear Paul McCartney going "bom bom bom ayeya" one more time, I'm going to open fire. It's true. Mark Chapman did get the wrong guy.

Jon Ronson (1992)

Bobby McFerrin
"Don't Worry, Be Happy"—A record that makes absolutely no attempt to address any of the problems it seeks to solve.

Peter Paphides (1994)

Meat Loaf (b 1947)
After the first album, Meat just lost it completely. Grunt! Grunt! Grunt! Grunt! I had to listen to that for nine months. That pig can't sing a f***ing note!

Jim Steinman (1989)

Freddie Mercury (of Queen) (1946–91)
"The Great Pretender" (1992)—Dead but still crap.

Jim Arundel

"The Freddie Mercury Album" (1992)—Mr. Teeth's solo hits "The Great Pretender" (early rock 'n' roll as glazed ham), "Love Kills" (electro-disco as melodrama), and "Barcelona" (opera as bollocks). You want the album for a Christmas present like you want a gift-wrapped box of verrucas. Let's face it, he was overrated and he wasn't that funny.

David Bennun

Ethel Merman (1909–84)
A chorus of taxi horns.

Anonymous

George Michael (b 1963)
Sleeping with George Michael would be like having sex with a groundhog.

Boy George

"Too Funky" (1992)—George has always managed to keep a hairy finger on the pulse of the moneyed wally.

Melody Maker

He's a wimp in disguise. He should go home and shave.

Keith Richards (1988)

Glenn Miller (1904–44)
Glenn should have lived, and the music should have died.

Al Klink

The Monkees
The Prefab Four.

Anonymous

First-grade music for kids in the first grade.

Mickey Dolenz

Jim Morrison (of the Doors) (1943–71)
On Oliver Stone's biopic The Doors *(1991)*—Do we need a two-and-half-hour movie about the Doors? I don't think so. I'll sum it up for you. I'M DRUNK—I'M NOBODY—I'M DRUNK—I'M FAMOUS—I'M DEAD. *Big Fat Dead Guy in a Bathtub,* there's your title.

Denis Leary

Van Morrison (b 1945)
"Days Like This"—It's everything you'd expect a Harry Connick Jr. album to be, and everything that you fear from an artist of Morrison's stature.

Ross Fortune (1995)

M People
"Bizarre Feast" (1994)—Functional music for middle-management types who had outgrown Phil Collins and wanted more street cred.

Peter Shapiro
Rock: The Rough Guide
(1996)

Willie Nelson

When you talk to him, he looks at you and grins and grins and nods and nods and appears to be the world's best listener, until you realize he is not listening at all.

Larry King

A lot of Americans don't think it's right that there are so many illegal immigrants roaming the countryside in rags and not paying taxes, because that's Willie Nelson's job.

Bill Maher
"Politically Incorrect" (1994)

New Kids on the Block

New Kids off the Production Line.

Andrew Burroughs (1990)

Red Nichols (1905–65)

Red thought he played like Bix Beiderbecke, but the similarity stopped the minute he opened his horn case.

Eddie Condon

Nirvana

I think Nirvana are a load of wop: biggest heap of crap I've ever seen. They're just lucky enough to have the money to sit around all day wearing sweaty check shirts.

Mark E. Smith (1993)

Jessye Norman (b 1945)

"Lucky to Be Me" (1992)—If you like this sort of thing, this is the sort of thing you like. I dread the appearance of "Jessye Sings Kylie Minogue."

Jeremy Beadle

Oasis

What a bunch of arseholes.

Wayne Fontana (1995)

Sinead O'Connor (b 1966)

A cow that can't sing.

Danny Baker

The bald-headed banshee.

London Sun *(1989)*

"Don't Cry for Me, Argentina" (1992)—The Ross Perot of pop. It's ugly.

Melody Maker

A gigantic, misguided ego.

New Musical Express

Sinead, thin voice and no hair, looks beautiful and sounds awful.

Time Out

The sweet-voiced Spamhead. . . . Talk about one track short of a compilation album.

Time Out

Shaquille O'Neal (b 1972)

"Kazam" (1996)—His dueling-rappers duet with the kid is the most excruciating musical [movie] interlude since Bruce Willis and Danny Aiello sang "Swinging on a Star" in *Hudson Hawk*.

Michael Sauter
Entertainment Weekly

Ozzy Osbourne (b 1948)

While you can't hold Ozzy responsible for the deaths of suicidal idiots, you can appreciate their motivation. I'd like to ensure I never have to hear him again, as well.

Mick Mercer

"Miracle Man" (1988)—The runoff groove on "Led Zeppelin II" sounds better than this offal.

Edwin Pouncey

Robert Palmer (b 1949)

"Ridin' High" (1992)—This is the night Palmer committed professional suicide.

Anonymous

Languid to the point of coma.

Ian Gittens

Luciano Pavarotti (b 1935)
"Don Carlos" (1992)—This evening Verdi is crying.

Anonymous heckler

A grotesque carnival king for the masses . . .
descending to the level of Madonna.

Corriere della Sera

"Il Trovatore"—He sounded so distant in the first act,
I thought he was phoning it in from Italy.

Manuel Hoeltherhoff
Wall Street Journal *(1988)*

Oscar Peterson (b 1925)
Fat, old, boring ivory-tinkler.

Spy *(1994)*

Pet Shop Boys
Music for malls and motorways.

Simon Frith (1990)

Tom Petty (b 1952)
"Free Fallin'" (1989)—Oh God, I've just played a
record written and produced by Jeff Lynne. No
wonder it's shite!

Ian McCann

"Free Fallin'" (1989)—Cowritten with ex-ELO man Jeff Lynne, which means one could scarcely take it less seriously if it had been cowritten with Jeffrey Archer.

David Stubbs

Pink Floyd

"The Wall"—This fourth-form philosophizing meanders across the fretboards of the consciousness, attempting to be Orwell, ending up being awful.

Melody Maker

"The Wall"—The last brick in Pink Floyd's own towering edifice. The rock musician's equivalent of the tired executive's toy, a gleaming, frivolous gadget that serves to occupy midspace. It's misplaced boredom.

New Musical Express *(1979)*

Police

If punk gave voice to the aimlessness of the first pessimistic postwar generation, then the Police were prime parasites of the new negativity.

Dave Hill

Elvis Presley (1935–77)

"Elvis over Easter" (1994)—A series of films on TV featuring the Burger King.

William Cook
Modern Review

After Presley appeared on "The Steve Allen Show"
(1956)—Unspeakable, untalented, and a vulgar young
entertainer.

> John Crosby

If Elvis had eaten green vegetables, he'd still be alive
today.

> Ian Dury

I'm not putting Elvis down, but he was a shitass, a
yellow belly, and I hated him, the f***er.

> Jerry Lee Lewis

Presley did not become a worthless shit: he always was
one.

> Charles Shaar Murray
> New Musical Express

Singing in any form is foreign to Elvis.

> Jack Payne (1956)

"Love Me Tender" (1956)—Is it a sausage? It is
certainly smooth and damp-looking. Is it a Walt
Disney goldfish? Is it a corpse? The face just hangs
there, limp and white with its little drop-seat mouth.
A peculiar sound emerges. A rusty foghorn? A voice?
Words occasionally can be made out: "Goan . . . git
. . . luhv."

> Time

(The Artist Formerly Known as) Prince (b 1958)
A toothpick in a purple doily.

Anonymous press review

"Purple Rain" (1984)—Ultimately as spineless as it
sounds.
Dave Hill

He is funky. Funky as a bucket of prawns in the sun.
Melody Maker *(1994)*

He's sort of a cross between Liberace and Johnny
Mathis.
Motion Picture Guide *(1984)*

"The Artist Currently Known as Unpronounceable"
has wasted too much time and public goodwill forcing
that damned symbol down our throats.

Rolling Stone *(1995)*

"Morning Papers" (1993)—Sounds like Michael
Jackson singing "We Are the World" with one arm
lifting a Slushy Pup, the other balancing a Parisian
cookbook. . . . Not a recommendation.

Everett True

Puff Daddy

"I'll Be Missing You" (1997)—This gives the lie to those who claim hip-hoppers are above self-serving sentimentality.

Tom Sinclair
Entertainment Weekly

Rayvon

"Some People"—The M.O.R. grooves . . . make Billy Ocean sound like a gangsta rapper.

Matt Diehl
Entertainment Weekly *(1997)*

Lou Reed (b 1942)

"Metal Machine Music" (1975)—One hour of nothing, absolutely nothing.

Lester Bangs

He looked, as ever, as cheerful as a tombstone.

Spencer Bright (1992)

Keith Richards (b 1943)

Even the deaf would be traumatized by prolonged exposure to the most hideous croak in Western culture. Richards's voice is simply horrible.

Nick Coleman

I'm glad I've given up drugs and alcohol. It would be awful to be like Keith Richards. He's pathetic. It's like a monkey with arthritis, trying to go on stage and look young. I have great respect for the Stones but they would have been better if they had thrown Keith out fifteen years ago.

Elton John

"Talk Is Cheap" (1988)—Talk is cheap, and this album is almost as worthless.

Terry Staunton

The Rolling Stones
They are called the ugliest group in Britain. They are not looked on very kindly by most parents, or by adults in general. They are even used to the type of article that asks big brother if he would let his sister go out with one of them.

London Mirror *(1964)*

"Mixed Emotions" (1988)—It's just turgid cack. Any pub band could have done it.

Graham Poppie

The "Greatest Rock 'n' Roll Band in the World" has made some of the lamest live albums in the world. Even as tour souvenirs, the albums have sounded, at worst, hollow . . . and, at best, inauthentic.

Rolling Stone *(1995)*
[Surely a case of biting the band that feeds it?]

I promise you they'll never be back on my show. I was shocked when I saw them.

Ed Sullivan (1964)

On Tin Machine's "Maggie's Farm" (1989)—This is a load of old tosh . . . Just what you'd imagine the Rolling Stones doing if they were still alive.

Everett True

Linda Ronstadt (b 1946)
"Dedicated to the One I Love" (1996)—Want to go to sleep? This album of rock classics sung as lullabies is just the ticket.

Bob Cannon
Entertainment Weekly

David Lee Roth (of Van Halen) (b 1955)
He comes on like a cross between a toreador and Miss World. Shortly after he opens his mouth, any critical response leaps into the foxhole and tries to come to terms with describing the indescribable.

Paul Mathur (1988)

William Shatner

"The Transformed Man"—His "Lucy in the Sky with Diamonds" is piss-yourself hilarious. . . . Instead of singing he declaims the lyrics as though they were the work of Shakespeare. . . . Most of the other tracks are Shakespearean speeches. . . . His Hamlet's not bad, but his Romeo sounds like a child molester and should be given a very wide berth.

David Cavannagh
Select *(1992)*

"The Transformed Man"—The track listings suggest Shatner might be short a dilithium crystal or two.

Time Out *(1992)*

Gene Simmons (of Kiss) (b 1949)

He looks like a goat that's OD'd on testosterone.

Melody Maker

Carly Simon (b 1945)

"You're So Vain"—If a horse could sing in a monotone, the horse would sound like Carly Simon, only a horse wouldn't rhyme yacht, apricot, and gavotte.

Robert Christgau

Simple Minds

"Glittering Prize: The Video" (1992)—Yes, at last the truth can be told. All along Simple Minds were really Genesis—with hair. For people who think that Hey-We'll-Do-the-Video-Right-Here-at-This-Gig promos are still a smooth idea.

Andrew Collis
Select

Frank Sinatra (1915–98)

"Live at the London Palladium" (1950)—You can hear every word he sings, which is sometimes a pity—considering his material. It is like being force-fed with treacle.

Anonymous

On Sinatra's seventy-fifth birthday concert at London's Royal Albert Hall—It was a sentimental rather than an inspiring evening, a ritual rather than a happening. . . . Time was in the wings, glancing at his watch.

George Melly
The Times *of London (1990)*

Heather Smith (of M People)

"Angel Street"—That awful barking girl-bloke mauls some vocals about love being nice.

Jane Bussmann
London Guardian *(1998)*

The Spice Girls

The Spice Girls are easier to tell apart than the Mutant
Ninja Turtles, but that is small consolation. . . . Let's
face it, the Spice Girls could be duplicated by any five
women under the age of thirty standing in line at
Dunkin' Donuts. . . . The Spice Girls have no
personalities, their bodies are carriers for inane chatter.

Roger Ebert
Chicago Sun-Times *(1998)*

The Spice Girls couldn't sing their way out of a latex
dress.

Troy Patterson
Entertainment Weekly *(1998)*

Why have these girls become such a hit??? Well, why
do whorehouses make money??? The only reason
whorehouses don't make more money than the Spice
Girls is because whorehouses are illegal.

Why We Hate the
Spice Girls *(1997)*

Bruce Springsteen (b 1949)

He plays four-and-a-half-hour sets. That's torture.
Does he hate his audience?

John Lydon (1989)

"Human Touch" *and* "Lucky Town" (1992)—Pub rock
on a NASA budget. . . . People like Bruce Springsteen
are slowly boring music to death.

> Melody Maker

He's the Walt Disney of street poets . . . as useful a
social commentator as Donald Duck.

> *Chris Rea*

"Human Touch" *and* "Lucky Town" (1992)—The
twenty-four songs here make up such a mixed bag that
you can't help wondering why the Boss didn't get off
the production line and take an interest in what was
happening over in quality control.

> *Robert Sandall*
> The Times *of London*

Dave Stewart (of the Eurythmics) (b 1952)
He must go down as one of the all-time biggest jokers
in pop history—from his beard to his part in foisting
the appalling Curve on an unsuspecting world. . . .
There should be a public health warning against the
man.

> *Mark Morris (1992)*

Rod Stewart (b 1945)
"Tom Trubert's Blues" (1992)—Rod sings Tom Waits.
Yeah, and I've been commissioned to make a new
recording of Richard Strauss's "Four Last Songs" by
Heinrich Goebbels.

> *Nick Coleman*

Stephen Stills (b 1945)
Good musician but bloody obnoxious. He makes more
enemies than friends.

> *Bill Wyman*
> *(of the Rolling Stones)*

Sting (b 1951)
A mega-bore on a huge scale.

> *Michael Heath*

"Russians" (1985)—Buy this and hear the most
fatuous, mock-innocent "concerned" pop song since
"I'd Like to Teach the World to Sing."

> *Dave Hill*

"Ten Summoner's Tales"—Doesn't it just make you
want to take the silly f***-wit outside and shoot him?

> Melody Maker *(1994)*

Sting—where is thy death?

> *Joe Queenan*
> If You're Talking to Me. . .
> *(1994)*

He sings like he wants to be a hungry African.

David Stubbs

Barbra Streisand (b 1942)
"Mother"—An unqualified bummer . . . in which she belts out the primal scream. A mechanized shriek that has all the humanity of a police siren, it makes an embarrassing mockery of a great song.

Stephen Holden
Rolling Stone

Her work is pretentiously arty, overinvolved, and overprojected, and made further intolerable by a vocal tone best described by the Irish word "keening."

John Indcox

"Higher Ground" (1997)—A collection of gruesomely pious songs that is probably best avoided on an empty stomach.

Peter Kane
Q *magazine (1998)*

She sings . . . acts . . . produces . . . and, at $350 a ticket, even scalps her own concerts.

Jim Mullen
People *(1994)*

"And Other Musical Instruments"—It is overproduced, overorchestrated and overbearing to the point of aesthetic nausea.

John O'Connor
New York Times *(1972)*

Dame Joan Sutherland (b 1926)
The ultimate purgatory would be to go to the Sydney Opera House and hear Joan Sutherland sing.

Kerry Packer (1977)

Art Tatum (1909–56)
From the first time you heard Art Tatum playing "Tea for Two," you've always felt that jazz is a dipshit idiom that chomps the big one.

Spy *(1994)*

Tony! Toni! Tone!
"Hits" (1997)—Chances are that, even if Tony! Toni! Tone! were working in your local 7–Eleven, you wouldn't know them from Adam. Or Addam. Or Adame.

Danny Scott
Q *magazine*

Pete Townshend (of The Who) (b 1945)
For the last twenty-three years he's been a constant embarrassment. There's nothing worse than a pub rocker with pretensions.

Jonh Wilde (1989)

The Traveling Wilburys

If Mozart were alive today, he'd still be too young to join the Traveling Wilburys.

> Bill Maher
> "Politically Incorrect" (1994)

Ruby Turner

"Motown Song Book" (1988)—The presence of the Temptations, Four Tops, Jimmy Ruffin, and Junior Walker on some tracks does little to improve matters; it's a bit like trying to put TCP on a gunshot wound.

> Terry Staunton

Steve Tyler (of Aerosmith)

He stands there groping himself, and he is forty-six years old. It disgusts me, but he tells me that the kids like it.

> Mia Tyler
> (his sixteen-year-old daughter)
> (1995)

U2

"Zoo TV" (1992)—What have zoos and U2 got in common, apart from the fact that enlightened people would like to abolish them and they're both full of shite?

> Mr. Agreeable

We could end up as awful as U2.

> Barney (of New Order) (1989)

"Zoo TV" (1992)—With its CNN outtakes and William Borroughs' cutups, "Zoo TV" began to look about as revolutionary as the outtakes from the Genesis video "Jesus, He Knows Me." . . . U2 have managed to do something no one thought possible—eradicate the memory of their "Rattle & Hum" image and replace it with one that is even more ridiculous.

Jim Shelley

If Jesus had seen U2 he would've been very mad indeed. Jesus would throw bottles at U2.

Mark E. Smith (1993)

Do you know who the most boring group in the world is? Give me Barry Manilow anytime.

Jim Steinman (1989)

"Desire" (1988)—Fellows have asked me for ten pence on streetcorners for more substantial musical fare.

David Stubbs

Ugly Kid Joe

"America's Least Wanted" (1992)—UKJ prove it's possible to be old enough to vote and still think it's funny to eat with your mouth open. This is average heavy rock with burping jokes to make up for lack of musical imagination.

Laura Lee Davies

Ugly Kid Joe are back. Presumably because scientists have yet to develop a vaccine.

Melody Maker (1994)

Urge Overkill

"Exit the Dragon" (1995)—Their happy-hour schtick and put-on rock-star airs have never been as funny or believable as the Urge themselves seem to think they are. . . . "Exit the Dragon" is mostly slow fizz with only intermittent sparkle.

Rolling Stone

Frankie Valli

When I hear the Four Seasons' "Walk Like a Man," I want to scream, "Frankie! SING like a man!"

Anonymous

Vanilla Ice (Robert Van Winkle)

Rap Van Winkle.

New Musical Express (1991)

Suzanne Vega

I could put on my Suzanne Vega tape and bore myself to death.

Sean Hughes (1990)

Village People

"Macho Man"—Lyrics so camp they have to be held down by tent pegs.

New Musical Express

Gene Vincent (1935–71)

"Be-Bop-A-Lula"—A junior idiot chant . . . strictly from the booby hatch.

New Musical Express (1956)

Paul Weller (of the Jam and Style Council) (b 1958)

There were actually three people in the Jam. And two of them weren't Paul Weller.

Bruce Foxton

He just stole everything. He's just a skinny twit who has the worst haircut going.

Ian McCulloch

Barry White (b 1944)

Barry White is a singer who turned black soul music into a product akin to soggy white blancmange. . . . His voice could be heard, grunting and gasping in a register of emotions from A to B flat . . . sounding as if somebody is throttling the vocalist with a pillow.

Philip Norman

Whitesnake

They only imagine they make a big noise and David Coverdale still believes he sounds like William Bell, which does not.

Ian McCann

The Who

"Tommy: The Rock Opera"—This stillborn, overanxious stretch of bilge. We needed rock opera like we needed rock Morris dancing.

Melody Maker

Jackie Wilson (1934–84)

"Reet Petite"—I thought the strange collection of noises, ranging from gargling to an outboard motor, was obviously Stan Freberg indulging in one of his satires.

Derek Johnson

The Wilsons

"Monday Without You" (1997)—The musical equivalent of carbon monoxide: tasteless, odorless, and deadly.

Wook Kim
Entertainment Weekly

Windham Hill record label

All that Windham Hill stuff—it's just music for the hot tub.

Anonymous phone-in listener
on WYNC radio (1984)

The Yardbirds

They want to play the blues so badly, and that's how they play it—badly!

Sonny Boy Williamson (1963)

Yes and Genesis

They are both as exciting as a used Kleenex.

Nick Lowe

6
FASHION

I never cared for fashion much—amusing little seams
and witty pleated skirts.

David Bailey (1990)

Half a dozen well-dressed men would be
indistinguishably alike if you decapitate them.
It is notorious that men are the slaves of fashion.

Arnold Bennett
The Meaning of Frocks
(1911)

American women mostly have their clothes arranged
for them. And their faces too, I think.

Noël Coward

You trying to ask me do I wear girdles and bras and
the rest of that junk? What do you think I am, a sissy?

Mildred "Babe" Didrickson

The fashion industry is largely run by men who
wouldn't know a real woman if they found one in
their black satin bedsheets.

Jill Parkin (1992)

Women who are not vain about their clothes are often
vain about not being vain about their clothes.

Cyril Scott

To call a fashion wearable is the kiss of death. No new
fashion worth its salt is ever wearable.

Eugenia Sheppard
New York Herald Tribune
(1960)

When seen in the perspective of half-a-dozen years or
more, the best of our fashions strike us as grotesque.

Thorstein Veblen
The Theory of the Leisure
Class (1899)

Far too much of a girl's time is taken up in dress.

Mary Wollstonecraft
Dress (circa 1780s)

CLOTHES AND ACCESSORIES

Animal Furs

It takes up to forty dumb animals to make a fur coat, but only one to wear it.

Bryn Jones

Artificial Fabrics

Polyester—the word that describes tacky for all time.

New York Times *(1991)*

Cosmetics

On opera singer Helen Traubel's wearing false eyelashes in Tristan and Isolde—It was like the Venus de Milo wearing a bra.

Philadelphia Inquirer

Hats

Her hat is a creation that will never go out of style. It will look ridiculous year after year.

Fred Allen

Is that a hat or a threat you're wearing?

Eddie Condon

On Queen Elizabeth II's collection of "bad hats"—She is not a fashion plate, she is a monarch. You can't have both.

Freddie Fox (1984)

Communists all seem to wear small caps, a look I consider better suited to tubes of toothpaste than people.

Fran Lebowitz
Metropolitan Life *(1978)*

For this lady, who had very black hair, had stuck over her right ear the pitiable corpse of a large white bird, which looked exactly as if someone had killed it by stamping on its breast, and then nailed it to the lady's temple, which was presumably of sufficient solidity to bear the operation.

George Bernard Shaw, letter (1905)

Jewelry

Don't ever wear artistic jewelry; it wrecks a woman's reputation.

Colette
Gigi *(1940)*

To a Pittsburgh Pirate teammate wearing three small gold chains around his neck—What's that? A Mr. T starter set?

Mike Diaz

On Bill Clinton's Iron Man Timex watch—Plastic digital, thick as a brick, and handsome as a hernia.

Gene Weingarten
Washington Post *(1993)*

Lingerie

I don't like those chiffon nighties—they show your vest.

Joyce Grenfell

I never could understand tennis players who wore nice dresses but showed dreary garments underneath.

Teddy Tinling

Men's Fashion

I want to know why, if men rule the world, they don't stop wearing neckties?

Linda Ellerbee
Move On: Adventures in
the Real World *(1991)*

Dressing a pool player in a tuxedo is like putting whipped cream on a hot dog.

Minnesota Fats

When someone in Green Bay says he has a good wardrobe, it means he has ten bowling shirts.

Greg Koch

I am not wearing bellbottoms again. I wore them once and I didn't get laid, all right?

Denis Leary
London Underground *(1992)*

Inflation is a man-made disaster . . . like Southern beer and nylon shirts.

Roland Long (1990)

On a badly fitting suit—It must have been made by the American Can Company.

James Thurber
Alarms and Diversions *(1957)*

To his football players—If you want to wear bellbottoms, join the navy; if you want long hair, become a hippie; if you want to wear a headband, get a job as an Indian in a movie.

Norm van Brocklin

Perfume
Giorgio perfume has a scent that even a truck driver with a head cold could pick out.

Anonymous in International Herald Tribune *(1992)*

It's hard to believe Sarah Ferguson's perfume deal fell through. Who wouldn't want to smell like a divorcée with money problems?

Jim Mullen
Entertainment Weekly *(1996)*

The new perfume Forever Krystle is like its namesake [Linda Evans's character in "Dynasty"], a bit too sweet, cloying, and only to be applied in very small amounts. In fact, a little squirt among perfumes.

Sue Peart

Shoes
If high heels were so wonderful, men would be wearing them.

Sue Grafton
I Is for Innocence *(1992)*

The trainer is the ugliest species of footwear ever devised.

"The Weasel"
London Independent *(1993)*

Wedding Dresses
Why should a sane, healthy woman be covered up in white gauze like the confectionery in a shop window when there are flies around?

H. G. Wells
Select Conversations *(1895)*

MODELS AND DESIGNERS

Supermodel? Don't you mean superficial?

Anjali (1994)

The provocative gyrations of women earning a crust on the catwalk in frocks that often seemed designed for the hooking and bondage classes.

Peter Dunn (1992)

It's been so cold on the East Coast, the goose bumps make some models look like they actually have breasts.

Jim Mullen
Entertainment Weekly *(1997)*

(Sir) Cecil Beaton (1904–80)
His baroque is worse than his bite.

Hank Brennan

Gabrielle "Coco" Chanel (1883–1971)
Chanel has never influenced fashion one bit.

Pierre Cardin

That damn bitch who sold the same jacket for thirty-five years!

Elsa Schiaparelli

Cindy Crawford

On the new Cindy doll—In the flesh, Cindy Crawford
is, inevitably, more plastic than perfect. Like her
Hasbro namesake, she seems so plastic and perfect I
had this insatiable urge to pull down her trousers to
see if she had any reproductive organs.

> *Nicole Davidson*
> Modern Review *(1992)*

Patti Davis *(Ronald Reagan's daughter)*

On Davis's nude photo shoot—She has donated half her
fee from *Playboy* to People for the Ethical Treatment
of Animals. It would be only fair, then, if an owl
donated its brain to her.

> *Richard Cohen*
> Washington Post *(1994)*

Christian Dior *(1905–57)*

I adore you, but you dress women like armchairs.

> *Coco Chanel*

On Dior's "New Look"—Look how ridiculous these
women are, wearing clothes by a man who doesn't
know women, never had one, and dreams of being
one.

> *Coco Chanel*

Jean-Paul Gaultier (b 1952)
Gandhi meets Amadeus on Carnaby Street.

Anonymous in New York
Times *(1993)*

Jerry Hall
Try interviewing her sometime. It's like talking to a window.

Bryant Gumbel

Karl Lagerfeld (b 1938)
His black mini topped by ankle-length chiffon is an idea that should have stayed in his sketchbook.

Lowri Turner
London Evening Standard
(1991)

Kate Moss
Nobody who isn't ill looks like that waif.

Naomi Wolf (1993)

Helena Rubinstein (1871–1965)
An old Polish frog with a huge casket of jewels.

Cecil Beaton

Yves Saint-Laurent (b 1936)
Saint-Laurent has excellent taste. The more he copies me, the better taste he displays.

Coco Chanel (1971)

Twiggy (Lesley Hornby)
Four straight limbs in search of a woman's body.

Newsweek (1967)

FASHION VICTIMS

On choosing his thirty-eighth annual worst-dressed list—
The final results of this year's list amply reflect the fact
that boring bombs, dowdy duds, and frumpy flops
continue to litter our landscape with wretched
regularity. To be honest, narrowing the couture-clad
fashion culprits down to a manageable group of ten
was almost as difficult as sitting through *The Postman*.

Mr. Blackwell (1998)

Today Hollywood film stars—even the real lookers
like Michelle Pfeiffer and Winona Ryder—are shy,
troubled creatures who dress like something Cat
Stevens dragged in from the local Saturday night
sackcloth-and-ashes hop.

Julie Burchill (1993)

Pamela Anderson (Lee)
Looks like a Martian Venus . . . in search of a shell.

Mr. Blackwell (1998)

Drew Barrymore

A tempest in a fleshpot.

Mr. Blackwell (1997)

Kim Basinger

This parading peep show should be banished to the bat cave.

Mr. Blackwell (1989)

Kathleen Battle

"A Carnegie Hall Christmas Concert" (1992)—
Kathleen Battle sang like an angel, but her dress
suggested she'd squeezed between two scarlet armchairs
and brought them with her.

Allison Pearson

Mr. Blackwell, fashion critic for *People*

The snobby fashion grouch.

Chicago Tribune (1998)

Cher

A bona-fide fashion fiasco—from nose to toe, she's the
tacky tattooed terror.

Mr. Blackwell (1991)

A Hawaiian bar mitzvah.

Mr. Blackwell

On Cher's costume at the 1986 Oscars ceremony—
An X-rated impersonation of a '56 Pontiac hood
ornament.

Newsweek

The first time I saw her I thought she was a hooker.

Phil Spector

Jill Clayburgh

She dresses like an African bush waiting for a safari.

Mr. Blackwell

Bill Clinton

Clinton plays golf: he wore jogging shoes, and his shirt
was hanging out over painter's pants. Golf needs
Clinton like it needs a case of ringworm.

Rick Reilly
Sports Illustrated *(1992)*

Have you ever seen how he dresses to jog? He wears
what looks like a pair of Babe Ruth's old swimming
trunks and a P.E.-issue plain gray T-shirt. I mean, I
still believe in a place called Hope—unless it's where
he shops for jogging clothes.

Rick Reilly
Sports Illustrated *(1992)*

Glenn Close

After Close's appearance as Cruella DeVille—Forget the Dalmatians, Glenn should be starring in *101 Fashion Frustrations.* It's doggone depressing.

Mr. Blackwell (1997)

On her appearance as Norma Desmond in Sunset Boulevard—Anthony Powell's extravagantly ugly costumes don't help—they make her look like a drag queen. In one scene she sports a leopardskin gown accordioned out like something from before the Civil War.

Steve Vineberg
Modern Review *(1994)*

Joan Collins

A hymn to overstatement if ever there was one.

Mr. Blackwell

Claire Danes

On screen her Juliet is pure Shakespearean magic; off screen her fad-mad monstrosities are perfectly tragic.

Mr. Blackwell (1997)

Geena Davis

At the 1992 Oscars ceremony—The Oscar for the Most
Audacious Frock definitely went to Geena Davis,
whose white satin Bill Hargate gown looked like a
wedding dress from behind, a can-can outfit from in
front, and nothing on earth from the side.

The Times *of London*

Ellen DeGeneres

Throw those baggy fashion bombs back into the
closet.

Mr. Blackwell (1998)

John Foster Dulles, politician

He stirred whisky with a thick forefinger, his socks
drooped, his suits were green-hued, his ties were
indifferent, and his breath was chronically bad.
Hunched forward as he talked, he droned on in a flat
voice.

*Walter Isaacson
and Evan Thomas*

Queen Elizabeth II of England

An undeniably dull fish. Her dress sense—the epitome
of Drab Chic.

*Peter Freedman
Glad to Be Gray (1985)*

Sarah Ferguson, Duchess of York
Looks like an unemployed barmaid in search of a crown.

Mr. Blackwell (1997)

She is a lady short on looks, absolutely deprived of any dress sense, and has a figure like a Jurassic monster.

Nicholas Fairbairn

Goldie Hawn and Diane Keaton
Tinsel Town's Twin Titans of Tacky Taste strike again. Is it campy camouflage or simply self-sabotage?

Mr. Blackwell (1997)

Helen Hunt
A Twister has hit her. In those cutout catastrophes and peekaboo dreck, the Diva of Fashion Disaster resembles a twisted wreck.

Mr. Blackwell (1997)

Lisa Kudrow
Television's Friend is Fashion's Foe. When it comes to couture, she's a cavalcade of fashion woe.

Mr. Blackwell (1997)

David Letterman
As a guest on "The Late Show"—Who picks your clothes, Stevie Wonder?

Don Rickles (1996)

John Madden
John is one man who doesn't let success go to his clothes.

Mike Ditka

Madonna
She runs the gamut from Style Bore to Bumpy Bore. Let's be blunt, yesterday's Evita is today's Velveeta.

Mr. Blackwell (1998)

Marilyn Manson
He looks like Alice Cooper doing *Rosemary's Baby*.

Mr. Blackwell (1998)

Benito Mussolini
There is something wrong, even histrionically, with a man who wears white spats with a black shirt.

Ernest Hemingway
Toronto Daily Star *(1923)*

Martina Navratilova
In her leather-appliqued skirts and '70s wire-rim eyeglasses, she's the Tootsie of tennis.

Mr. Blackwell
Tennis *magazine (1990)*

Sinead O'Connor
A monastic monstrosity in baggy rags and combat boots—a creepy cross between Joan of Arc and Kojak.

Mr. Blackwell (1991)

Billy Packer, sportscaster
On Packer's new sports jacket—Who shot the couch?

Frank Glieber

Valerie Perrine
She looks like the Bride of Frankenstein doing the Ziegfeld Follies.

Mr. Blackwell

Lori Petty
A Technicolor nightmare, Miss Petty isn't pretty.

Mr. Blackwell (1997)

Raine, Countess Spencer, stepmother of Princess Diana
On Spencer's wedding to Count Jean-Francois de Chambrun—To call her a dog's dinner would be to provoke widespread outrage among canine nutritionists.

Anonymous (1993)

On Spencer's wedding—With cheeks the color of nuked tomatoes and a complexion like liberally floured tripe, the enduring impression of the countess was a rag doll careering at great speed through someone else's wash line.

Judy Rumbold (1993)

Ronald Reagan
One hesitates even to speculate about the polyester levels of his outfits. The dyed hair is an outrage, as is the rouge on the cheeks. (Will the president soon proceed to eye shadow and liner?)

Paul Fussell

Dennis Rodman
The Fashion Menace may be the Bad Boy of Basketball, but in fishnet and feathers, he's a unisex wreck.

Mr. Blackwell (1997)

He has so many fish hooks in his nose, he looks like a piece of bait.

Bob Costas

Beyond the hair, tattoos, and earrings, he's just like you and me.

Bob Hill (1995)

Elisabeth Shue

A positive Shue-in for Tomboy of the Year.

Mr. Blackwell (1997)

The Spice Girls

Five candy-colored beauties trapped in fashion waste
. . . the only spices on the planet that have no taste!

Mr. Blackwell (1998)

The Spice Girls attired, as usual, like cartoon call girls.

Troy Patterson
Entertainment Weekly *(1998)*

Girl Power is showing cleavage and wearing short
skirts while taking money out of one hand and putting
a lame cassette in the other hand of googly-eyed old
people. . . . Girl Power is a struggle to always look
good and to find the right accessories to go with that
Union Jack miniskirt!

Why We Hate the
Spice Girls *(1997)*

Star Trek

The USS *Enterprise* crew's tacky uniforms still look like
pajamas and Kirk, with open collar jauntily flapping,
looks like he's wearing upside-down Dr. Dentons.

Motion Picture Guide

Barbra Streisand

She looks like the masculine Bride of Frankenstein.

Mr. Blackwell

Elizabeth Taylor

Elizabeth Taylor is wearing Orson Welles' designer jeans.

Joan Rivers

Ivana Trump

A middle-aged laughingstock, a matron desperately in search of a career after being dumped for this year's model.

Julie Burchill (1992)

Diana Vreeland

She had rouged cheeks of a color otherwise seen on specially ordered Pontiac Firebirds, and in her ears she wore two feathered appliances resembling surfcasting jigs especially appetizing to a striped bass.

George V. Higgins
Wall Street Journal *(1984)*

Orson Welles

He was clad in a black blimp cleverly painted to look like a dinner jacket.

Clive James (1980)

Mae West

She was dressed in a peignoir of beige lace, with a blonde wig above false eyelashes—a kind of Mount Rushmore of the cosmetician's art.

Dwight Whitney (1965)

Vanna White

Mall fashions at their worst.

Mr. Blackwell

7
BOOKS AND
WRITERS

Many authors, when one meets them for the first time, are comparatively unimpressive compared to their books.

John Betjeman

Science fiction, like Brazil, is where the nuts come from.

Thomas M. Disch (1987)

You certainly wouldn't turn to contemporary poets for guidance in the twentieth-century world.

Northrop Frye (1963)

The shelf life of a modern hardback writer is somewhere between milk and yoghurt.

John Mortimer (1987)

All writers are vain, selfish, and lazy, and at the very
bottom their motives are a mystery.

> *George Orwell*

Writing is not a profession, but a vocation of
unhappiness. . . . Literature with a capital *L* is rubbish.

> *Georges Simenon*

American writers want to be not good but great; and
so are neither.

> *Gore Vidal*
> Two Sisters

"American dry goods? What are they, I wonder?"
enquired Lord Henry. "American novels?"

> *Oscar Wilde*
> The Picture of Dorian Gray

Alice Adams (b 1926)
While I admire the cool surfaces of Alice Adams's
stories, they leave me wanting more heat.

> *Ron Carlson*
> New York Times
> Book Review *(1989)*

Glenda Adams (b 1939)

Games of the Strong (1989)—What audience is going to be captivated by a passive, jinxed, self-despising female nerd?

> *John Tranter*
> American Book Review

Louisa May Alcott (1832–88)

She preserved to the age of fifty-six that contempt for ideas which is normal among boys and girls of fifteen.

> *Odell Shepherd*
> North American Review

Steve Allen (b 1921)

Steve Allen on the Bible, Religion, and Morality (1990)— This work is so relentlessly belligerent that one is not surprised to find that he originally planned to publish it posthumously.

> *Richard S. Watts*
> Literary Journal

Kingsley Amis (1922–95)

An overestimated writer affecting the high social style of club curmudgeon.

> *Saul Bellow*

Martin Amis (b 1949)
The Information (1995)—Mr. Amis is his generation's
top literary dog . . . highly pedigreed, but his terrain is
the junkyard of the human psyche.

> *Christopher Buckley*
> New York Times

Isaac Asimov (1920–92)
Nemesis (1989)—Reads more like an outline for an
Asimov novel.

> *Gerald Jonas*
> New York Times
> Book Review

Margot Asquith (1864–1945)
Re-Enter Margot Asquith—This book of essays . . . has
all the depth and glitter of a worn dime.

> *Dorothy Parker*
> New Yorker *(1927)*

W. H. Auden (1907–73)
He wound up as a poor old fag at bay,
Beleaguered in the end as at the start
By dons appalled that he could talk all day
And not draw breath although pissed as a fart.

> *Clive James (1992)*

There is a terrible weightlessness behind Auden's
brilliance from which all his wit and erudition cannot
save him.

> *Lawrence Norfolk*
> Times Literary Supplement
> *(London) (1991)*

Jane Austen (1775–1817)

If Jane Austen were alive today she'd probably be
writing books called things like *Sex and Sensibility* and
Pride and Passion.

> *Julie Burchill*
> Modern Review *(1992)*

I am at a loss to understand why people hold Miss
Austen's novels at so high a rate, which seem to me
vulgar in tone, sterile in artistic invention, imprisoned
in the wretched conventions of English society,
without genius, wit, or knowledge of the world.
Never was life so pinched and narrow.

> *Ralph Waldo Emerson*
> Journal *(1861)*

Jane Austen's books, too, are absent from this library.
Just that one omission alone would make a fairly good
library out of a library that hadn't a book in it.

> *Mark Twain*
> Follow the Equator

Paul Auster (b 1947)

Leviathan (1992)—It may start with a bang, but
Leviathan finishes with the sound of someone simply
banging on.

Tom Shone (1992)

James Baker (b 1930)

The Politics of Diplomacy (1995)—Baker's
misunderstanding of the disintegration of the Soviet
Empire is perhaps the most impressive part of his
memoirs.

Michael Ledeen
National Review

J. G. Ballard (b 1930)

Crash—The author of this book is beyond psychiatric
help.

Anonymous publisher (1973)

Rushing to Paradise (1995)—It is a nasty and utterly
humorless book.

George Needham
Booklist

Charles Barkley (b 1963)

Outrageous! (autobiography) (1992)—Once you put it
down, you can't pick it up. Its chief fault is the covers
are too far apart.

Pat Williams

Joel Barlow (1754–1812)
No poet with so little of poetry ever received so much glory.

> *Fred L. Pattee*
> The First Century of
> American Literature *(1935)*

Simone de Beauvoir (1908–86)
Mlle. de Beauvoir is a plodder par excellence. Not for her the masterstroke which cuts a long story short; she opts every time for the Long March—the long plod.

> *Brigid Brophy*
> New York Times *(1965)*

Samuel Beckett (1906–89)
Molloy; Malone Dies; The Nameable (1959)—The suggestion that something larger is being said about the human predicament won't hold water, any more than Beckett's incontinent heroes can.

> The Spectator

Peter Benchley (b 1940)
The Deep—A woefully crummy book.

> *Russell Davies*

Robert Benchley (1889–1945)
An enchanting toad of a man.

> *Helen Hayes*

Dorothy Parker regarded him as a slice of packaged
white bread: unambiguous and predictable.

Marion Meade
Dorothy Parker *(1988)*

Anthony Bianco (b 1953)
Rainmaker (1991)—Mr. Bianco recently condensed the
essential elements of his [486-page] book into twelve
pages for *New York* magazine. The sad part is nothing
of significance was lost.

Kurt Eichenwald
New York Times
Book Review

Victor Bockris (b 1948)
Keith Richards (biography) (1992)—Keith Richards
comes across as a decent man, but . . . reading about a
junkie—even a junkie who played guitar on "Jumping
Jack Flash"—is depressing and dull. . . . It is as lopsided
as the other partisan biography, *Diana—Her True Story,*
with Mick Jagger cast as the Prince of Wales.

Tony Parsons

Anne Brontë (1820–49)
The Tenant of Wildfell Hall (1848)—The scenes which
the heroine relates in her diary are of the most
disgusting and revolting species.

The Rambler *(1848)*

Charlotte Brontë (1816–55)

Jane Eyre (1847)—Blatantly such stuff as daydreams are made on. Reading *Jane Eyre* is like gobbling a jar full of schoolgirl stickjaw.

> *Brophy, Levey, and Osborne*
> 50 Works of Literature We
> Could Do Without *(1967)*

There is no longer any doubt that the public is threatened with an infinite series of novels of a new class, which will be strung on, like the knotted tail of a kite, to the popular work *Jane Eyre*. . . . The mind that conceived them is one of great strength and fervor but coarse almost to the point of brutality.

> The Literary World *(1848)*

Emily Brontë (1818–48)

Wuthering Heights (1847)—Wild, confused, disjointed, and improbable.

> The Examiner

Wuthering Heights (1847)—A particularly lackluster contribution to the literature not of domestic terror but of the terror of domesticity.

> *David Pascoe*
> Literary Review *(1992)*

Robert Browning (1812–89)
McCay was of a romantic and sentimental nature. The sort of man who . . . knew Ella May Wilcox by heart, and could take Browning without anaesthetics.

P. G. Wodehouse
The Man Upstairs *(1914)*

Pearl Buck (1892–1973)
Oh, poor Pearl Buck! No more bounce than a boiled potato!

Katherine Anne Porter

Anthony Burgess (1917–93)
He is like someone on a quiz show who insists on giving answers in greater detail than is actually necessary.

William Leith (1989)

William Burroughs (1914–97)
The works of William Burroughs add up to the world's pluperfect put-on.

Time

Barbara Bush (b 1925)
A Memoir (1994)—One of the dullest memoirs ever to lay waste to a forest.

Frank Rich
New York Times

Lord Byron (1788–1824)

Don Juan—It is indeed truly pitiable to think that one of the greatest poets of the age should have written a poem that no respectable bookseller could have published without disgracing himself—but a work so atrocious must not be suffered to pass into oblivion without the infliction of that punishment on its guilty author due to such wanton outrage on all most dear to human nature.

Blackwood's (1819)

Hours of Idleness (1807)—We counsel him to forthwith abandon poetry. . . . He is at best an intruder in the groves of Parnassus.

Henry Brougham
The Edinburgh Review

Michael Caine (b 1933)

What's It All About? (autobiography) (1992)—He writes like he acts, with yawning monotony.

Simon Garfield

Lady Colin Campbell (b 1949)

Diana in Private (1992)—She calls herself a royal confidante, but I doubt if she could spot Princess Diana in a police lineup. She is a female Walter Mitty. Her book is fantasy, fabrication, and fatuousness. It is bile, laced with bitchiness and layered with vitriol.

Anonymous
London Daily Mail

Naomi Campbell (b 1970)

Swan (1994)—If this novel were a model, she'd be lame, clumsy, and grasping, with bulges in all the wrong places.

Susannah Herbert

Albert Camus (1913–60)

The Fall (1957)—The style is unattractive if apt, being the oblique stilted flow of a man working his way round to asking for a loan.

Anthony Quinton
New Statesman

Truman Capote (1924–84)

In Cold Blood (1965)—A failure of the imagination.

Norman Mailer (1965)

He's a full-fledged housewife from Kansas with all the prejudices.

Gore Vidal

On hearing of Capote's death—Good career move.

Gore Vidal (1984)

Louis-Ferdinand Céline (1894–1961)

Journey to the End of the Night (1934)—Most readers will find this a revolting book; its vision of human life will seem to them a hideous nightmare. . . . If this is life, then it is better not to live.

> *J. D. Adams*
> New York Times
> Book Review

(Dame) Agatha Christie (1890–1976)

Her stories are puzzles, not novels. The characters aren't even lifelike enough to be caricatures. I don't like Agatha Christie at all.

> *Ruth Rendell (1992)*

On Christie's character Miss Marple—A horrible old village spinster . . . a tiresome busybody.

> *Ruth Rendell (1992)*

Tom Clancy (b 1947)

All Clancy's characters sound exactly the same.

> *Paul Gray*
> Time *(1991)*

The Sum of All Fears (1991)—A whizz-bang page-turner, but to be honest not all the pages get read.

> *Morton Kondracke*
> New York Times
> Book Review

James Clavell (1925–94)

Whirlwind (1986)—It makes a lovely doorstop!

> Everett Groseclose
> Wall Street Journal

Jackie Collins (b 1937)

Lady Boss (1990)—The most awful book I have ever reviewed. The prose is banal . . . and the many bursts of sexual activity have the quality of short-time couplings in a brothel. One weeps for the noble trees that had to be pulped to enable this concoction to be published.

> Anthony Looch

Joan Collins (b 1933)

Prime Time (1988)—I couldn't believe my eyes when I started to read this sordid attempt at authorship. It sickened me—it's quite evil in the debauchery it portrays.

> Barbara Cartland

Michael Crichton (b 1942)

Disclosure (1994)—The current king of crummy novelization is Michael Crichton. . . . *Disclosure* is a 400-page inkblot.

> Allen Barra
> Modern Review

Charles Darwin (1809–82)
The Origin of Species (1859)—A brutal philosophy—to
wit, there is no God, and the ape is our Adam.

Cardinal Manning

The Origin of Species (1859)—I started *Origin of Species*
today, but it's not as good as the television series.

Sue Townsend
The Secret Diary of
Adrian Mole *(1982)*

Len Deighton (b 1929)
Spy Sinker (1990)—Len Deighton has exhausted the
cold war as a lively topic in the twenty-eight years and
twenty-odd books he's written. *Spy Sinker* suggests the
topic also has exhausted him.

Morton Kondracke
New York Times
Book Review

Ethel M. Dell (1881–1939)
She rode the trash-horse hell-for-leather.

Rose Macaulay

Jane DeLynn (b 1946)

Don Juan in the Village (1990)—Again and again, it made me feel like a bartender with a single customer and a long night ahead.

Bertha Harris
New York Times
Book Review

Charles Dickens (1812–70)

The Pickwick Papers (1836)—Mr. Dickens writes too often and too fast. If he persists much longer in this course, it requires no gift of prophecy to foretell his fate—he has risen like a rocket, and he will come down like a stick.

Anonymous (1838)

We were all put to Dickens as children but it never quite took. That unremitting humanity soon had me cheesed off.

Alan Bennett

A Tale of Two Cities (1859)—It was a sheer dead pull from start to finish. It all seemed so sincere, such a transparent make-believe, a mere piece of acting.

John Burroughs
Century *(1897)*

A totally disinherited waif.

George Santayana

Hard Times (1854)—On the whole, the story is stale, flat, and unprofitable: a mere dull melodrama, in which character is caricature, sentiment tinsel, and moral (if any) unsound.

> *Richard Simpson*
> The Rambler *(1854)*

The Pickwick Papers (1836)—The general theory of life on which it is based is not only false, but puerile. Fifty years hence most of his wit will be harder to understand than the allusions in the *Dunciad;* and our grandchildren will wonder what their ancestors could have meant by putting Mr. Dickens at the head of the novelists of his day.

> *James F. Stephens*
> Saturday Review *(1858)*

Emily Dickinson (1830–86)

An eccentric, dreamy, half-educated recluse in an out-of-the-way New England village (or anywhere else) cannot with impunity set at defiance the laws of gravitation and grammar. Oblivion lingers in the immediate neighborhood.

> *Thomas B. Aldrich*
> Atlantic Monthly *(1892)*

J. P. Donleavy (b 1926)
The Ginger Man (1955)—This rather nasty, rather
pompous novel gives us, in all, a precocious small boy's
view of life, the boy having been spoiled somehow
and allowed to indulge in sulks and tantrums and
abundant self-pity.

Chicago Tribune *(1958)*

John Dos Passos (1896–1970)
The 42nd Parallel (1930)—He is like a man who is
trying to run in a dozen directions at once, succeeding
thereby merely in standing still and making a noise.

V. S. Pritchett
The Spectator

Norman Douglas (1868–1952)
A mixture of Roman emperor and Roman cab driver.

Reginald Turner

Theodore Dreiser (1871–1945)
An American Tragedy (1925)—His style, if style it may
be called, is offensively colloquial, commonplace, and
vulgar.

Boston Evening Transcript

An Indiana peasant, snuffling absurdly over imbecile
sentimentalities, giving a grave ear to quackeries,
snorting and eye-rolling with the best of them. . . .
He is still in the transition stage between Christian
Endeavor and civilization.

H. L. Mencken

Mr. Theodore Dreiser's book about himself sounds like
nothing but a loud, human purr.

Agnes Repplier

George Eliot (1819–80)
The Mill on the Floss (1860)—The hideous trans-
formation by which Maggie is debased . . . would
probably and deservedly have been resented as a brutal
and vulgar outrage on the part of a male novelist. . . .
It is a radical and mortal plague-spot, corrosive and
incurable.

Algernon Swinburne (1877)

T. S. Eliot (1888–1965)
The Waste Land (1922)—Unintelligible, the
borrowings cheap and the notes useless.

F. L. Lucas
New Statesman *(1923)*

Brett Easton Ellis (b 1964)
Ellis is about fifteen, isn't he?

Martin Amis (1988)

American Psycho (1991)—It reads like an endless brand-name catalogue.

> *John Heilpern*

American Psycho (1991)—Every bad thing you have read about this book is an understatement. It's ineptly written. It's sophomoric. It is, in the truest sense of the word, obscene. . . . It would take more space than the task deserves to catalog all of Ellis's myriad ineptnesses.

> *Terry Teachout*
> National Review

American Psycho (1991)—The single most boring book I have ever had to endure. Imagine a Dantesque circle devoted to the sin of name-dropping.

> *Naomi Wolf*
> New Statesman

Ralph Waldo Emerson (1803–82)
Belongs to a class of gentlemen with whom we have no patience whatever—the mystics for mysticism's sake.

> *Edgar Allan Poe (1842)*

Emerson's writing has a cold, cheerless glitter, like the new furniture in a warehouse, which will come of use by and by.

> *Alexander Smith*
> Dreamthorp *(1864)*

William Faulkner (1897–1962)

He was a great friend of mine. Well, as much as you could be a friend of his, unless you were a fourteen-year-old nymphet.

Truman Capote

Even those who call Mr. Faulkner our greatest literary sadist do not fully appreciate him, for it is not merely his characters who have to run the gauntlet but also his readers.

Clifton Fadiman

Edna Ferber (1887–1968)

Ice Palace—This book, which is going to be a movie, has the plot and character of a book which is going to be a movie.

Dorothy Parker
Esquire *(1958)*

Henry Fielding (1707–54)

Tom Jones (1749)—Vicious. . . . I scarcely know a more corrupt work.

Samuel Johnson

Carrie Fisher (b 1956)

Surrender the Pink (1990)—Fisher often writes scenes as if she knows her agent is shopping the movie rights.

Cathleen McGuigan
Newsweek

Surrender the Pink (1990)—It is utterly unmemorable.

> John Skow
> Time

F. Scott Fitzgerald (1896–1940)
The Great Gatsby (1925)—A little slack, a little soft, more than a little artificial. *The Great Gatsby* falls into the class of negligible novels.

> Springfield Republican

Ford Madox Ford (1873–1939)
What he really is or if he is really, nobody knows now and he least of all. . . . He is a system of assumed personas.

> *H. G. Wells*

Sigmund Freud (1856–1939)
Moses and Monotheism (1939)—This book is poorly written, full of repetitions, replete with borrowings from unbelievers, and spoiled by the author's aesthetic bias and his flimsy psycho-analytic fancies.

> Catholic World

Betty Friedan (b 1921)
The Feminine Mystique (1963)—The very Chateau Lafite of whine.

> *Michael Elliot*
> Newsweek *(1994)*

Robert Frost (1874–1963)
A nice, acrid, savage, pathetic old chap.

I. A. Richards

André Gide (1869–1951)
An unattractive man with a pale-green complexion.

Steven Runciman

What a strange and hollow talent! Gide appears to be completely indifferent to human nature, none of his characters have character, and he hangs bits of behavior on them just as one hung different paper hats on flat paper mannequins.

Sylvia Townsend Warner

Allen Ginsberg (b 1926)
That beard in search of a poet.

Caesar Bottom

William Golding (1911–93)
After Golding won the 1983 Nobel Prize for Literature—
A little English phenomenon of no special interest.

Artur Lundkvist
(a Nobel judge)

Albert Goldman (b 1931)
Elvis (biography)—The book is a prodigy of bad
writing, excitable, sarcastic, and only fleetingly literate.
It is also as exploitive as the exploiters whom Goldman
reviles, and no more tasteful than an Elvis jumpsuit.

Martin Amis

The Lives of John Lennon (biography) (1988)—Goldman
is a body snatcher. John has been assassinated and now
he's been crucified.

Cynthia Lennon

Germaine Greer (b 1939)
A bag of nutty slack.

Julie Burchill

An evil, rude, malicious bat.

Richard Ingram (1993)

The Female Eunuch (1970)—Ego-serving, malignant,
posturing, and false.

Neil Lyndon
No More Sex War *(1992)*

The Female Eunuch (1970)—Her book reads like nothing
so much as the wild cries of a woman at bay.

Malcolm Muggeridge
Things Past *(1978)*

John Grisham (b 1955)
The Chamber (1994)—Reading it is like hearing a young and pedestrian barrister opening a case to a bored jury on a dull day in court.

> *John Mortimer*
> The Times *of London*

Thomas Hardy (1840–1928)
The best prose is usually written by poets—Shakespeare wrote the best seventeenth century, and Shelley the best nineteenth; and I don't think I'm going too far when I say that Mr. Hardy has written the worst.
> *George Moore*

The Return of the Native (1878)—We maintain that the primary object of a story is to amuse us, and in the attempt to amuse us Mr. Hardy breaks down.

> Saturday Review

Joseph Heller (b 1923)
Catch 22 (1961)—The book is an emotional hodgepodge.

> New York Times Book
> Review

Lillian Hellman (1907–84)
Every word she writes is a lie, including *and* and *the*.

> *Mary McCarthy*

Ernest Hemingway (1899–1961)
A Farewell to Arms (1929)—A footnote to the minor
art of Gertrude Stein, an appendix to the biography of
the great novelist Scott Fitzgerald, and the Ouida of
the thirties.

> *Brophy, Levey, and Osborne*
> 50 Works of Literature We
> Could Do Without *(1967)*

For Whom the Bell Tolls (1940)—Mr. Hemingway . . .
please leave stories of the Spanish Civil War to
Malraux.

> Commonweal

The Sun Also Rises (1926)—His characters are as
shallow as the saucers in which they stack their daily
emotions.

> The Dial

He got hold of the red meat of the English language
and turned it into hamburger.

> *Richard Gordon*

I read him for the first time in the early 1940s,
something about bells, balls, and bulls . . . and I
loathed it.

> *Vladimir Nabokov*

Katharine Hepburn (b 1907)

Me: Stories of My Life (autobiography)—The rampant
egotism implied by the title is all too painfully
prominent throughout this "long-awaited memoir."
Less embarrassing than having to watch her tremulous
"nodding dog" television interviews.

Time Out

Shere Hite (b 1942)

The Hite Report on Female Sexuality—Masters and
Johnson with a dab of perfume behind the labia. . . .
Clotted-cream soft porn for women who don't want to
be caught with the real thing.

Anonymous American historian

Sheer hype is what American academics call her. Here
they prefer the nickname "Sheer Shite."

London Observer *(1994)*

Gerard Manley Hopkins (1844–89)

Poems—The poetry of a mental cripple.

Brophy, Levey, and Osborne
50 Works of Literature We
Could Do Without *(1967)*

A. E. Housman (1859–1936)

A Shropshire Lad (1896)—As far as writing *A Shropshire
Lad*, I shouldn't have thought A. E. Housman capable
of reading it.

Anonymous

Arianna S. Huffington (b 1950)

Her pearly teeth: no stains or chips . . . which is remarkable given that they have bitten off more than they can chew.

Robert Hughes
Time *(1988)*

Aldous Huxley (1894–1963)

Point Counter Point (1928)—He writes in the half clinical, half with-genteel-attention-averted manner of someone obliged to clean the lavatory.

Brophy, Levey, and Osborne
50 Works of Literature We
Could Do Without *(1967)*

Brave New World (1932)—A lugubrious and heavy-handed piece of propaganda.

New York Herald-Tribune

Henry James (1843–1916)

He was like a butler listening at the keyhole to hear what the Duchess and the Duke were saying to each other.

W. Somerset Maugham

A little emasculated mass of inanity.

Theodore Roosevelt

He talked as if every sentence had been carefully rehearsed; every semicolon, every comma, was in exactly the right place, and his rounded periods dropped on the floor and bounced about like tiny rubber balls.

Alfred Sutro

Michael Johnson
Slaying the Dragon (autobiography) (1996)—There isn't a single sentence in it that couldn't have been lifted intact from the children's book *The Little Engine Who Knew Too Much*.

Gene Lyons
Entertainment Weekly

James Jones
If James Jones, who is a fourth-rate writer . . . is worth three-quarters of a million, then I must be worth Fort Knox.

Nelson Algren, on Jones's
large book advance

James Joyce (1882–1941)
Ulysses (1922)—The telephone directory is, because of its rigorous selection and repression, a work of art compared to a wastepaper basket. And *Ulysses* is a wastepaper basket.

Glenn Gould
The English Novel of Today
(1924)

Probably Joyce thinks that because he prints all the dirty little words he is a great novelist.

George Moore

Ulysses (1922)—Written by a man with a diseased mind and soul so black he would even obscure the darkness of Hell.

Reed Smoot (senator)

M. M. Kaye (b 1909)
The Far Pavilions (1978)—One of those big, fat paperbacks intended to while away a monsoon or two. . . . If thrown with a good overarm action, it will bring a water buffalo to its knees.

Nancy Banks-Smith

John Keats (1795–1821)
Keats wrote indecently, probably in the indulgence of his social propensities.

Blackwood's
(obituary) (1821)

That dirty little blackguard Keats . . . .

Lord Byron

Collected Works—Fricassee of dead dog.

Thomas Carlyle

Kitty Kelley (b 1942)
Nancy Reagan (biography) (1991)—Today's mud is
served on fancy china at the Four Seasons.

> Newsweek

Nancy Reagan (1991)—Should this book be taken
seriously? Perhaps, but only by people who can shine a
flashlight directly through one ear and have light come
out the other.

> *Joe Queenan*
> New York Review of Books

Ms. Kelley, sixtysomething, blonde meringue hairdo,
five foot nothing and from Texas . . . looks as if she
played Charlene Tilton's grandmother in "Dallas."

> *Anne Robinson*
> The Times *of London (1994)*

His Way (Frank Sinatra biography) (1986)—I hope the
next time she crosses the street four blind guys come
along driving cars.

> *Frank Sinatra*
>
> [One of Sinatra's PR aides called
> Kelley "modern mudslinging's
> minuscule mistress of malice."]

Frank Kermode (b 1919)
A jumped-up, book-drunk ponce.

> *Philip Larkin, letter*

Ronald Kessler (b 1943)
Inside the White House (1995)—He shows Bill Clinton
as such a womanizer as to make Jack Kennedy seem
celibate.

Publishers Weekly

Stephen King (b 1947)
Rose Madder (1995)—The suspense soon gives way to
silliness, and it's harder to ignore King's bedrock of
vulgarity.

David Gates
Newsweek

Everyone knows Stephen King's flaws: tone-deaf
narration, papier-mâché character, clichés, gratuitous
vulgarity, self-indulgent digressions.

Andy Solomon
New York Times
Book Review

Rudyard Kipling (1865–1936)
Kipling is a jingo imperialist, he is morally insensitive
and aesthetically disgusting.

George Orwell

Ed Koch (b 1924)

Murder at City Hall (1995)—There's not much to recommend this self-promoting, full-of-itself book, thinly disguised as a mystery, other than the fact that it was written by "Hizzoner," the former mayor of New York.

> *Emily Melton*
> Booklist

Mayor (1984)—Koch has committed egocide with this book.

> *Jack Newfield*
> People

Dean Koontz (b 1945)

The Dark Symphony (1970)—It's unabashed trash and will do to prop up a table leg.

> *Joanna Russ*
> Magazine of Fantasy and
> Science Fiction *(1971)*

Judith Krantz (b 1927)

Scruples Two (1992)—When we are told that *Scruples* is "the story that millions of readers never wanted to end," I think we can safely take that one with a fair-sized Siberian salt mine.

> *Julie Burchill*
> Modern Review *(1992)*

Princess Daisy—As a work of art, it has the same status as a long conversation between two not very bright drunks.

Clive James

Howard Kurtz (b 1953)
Media Circus (1993)—Mr. Kurtz's heart is probably in the right place. It's just that his brain sometimes goes AWOL.

Joe Queenan
Wall Street Journal

D. H. Lawrence (1885–1930)
Filth. Nothing but obscenities.

Joseph Conrad

During the trial of Penguin Books and Lady Chatterley's Lover *under the Obscene Publications Act*—Would you approve of your young sons, young daughters . . . reading this book? Is it a book that you would leave lying around your own house? Is it a book that you would wish your wives or your servants to read?

Mr. Griffith-Jones
(prosecution counsel) (1960)

He looked like a plaster goose on a stone toadstool . . . a bad self-portrait by Van Gogh.

Edith Sitwell
Taken Care of *(1965)*

The Plumed Serpent (1926)—If this writing up of a
new faith is intended for a message, then it is only a
paltry one, with its feathers, its bowls of human blood,
and its rhetoric.

> The Spectator

T. E. Lawrence (1888–1935)
If he hides in a quarry he puts red flags all around.

> *George Bernard Shaw*

Warren Leamon
Unkind Melodies (1990)—It does not, as the title
borrowed from Keats suggests, capture the tunes of
pipers forever young. Rather, it sounds like the notes
of a transient player whistling "Dixie" out of tune.

> *Shelby Hearon*
> New York Times
> Book Review

Timothy Leary (1920–96)
His ashes were shot into space. So his body and brain
could finally be together after all these years.

> *Jim Mullen*
> Entertainment Weekly *(1997)*

John Le Carré (b 1931)
The Spy Who Came in from the Cold (1963)—You're
welcome to Le Carré—he hasn't got any future.

> *Anonymous publisher (1963)*

The Secret Pilgrim (1991)—Little more than a loose bit of string to tie various good ideas for stories that never made it into his other books.

> Ian Buruma
> New York Times
> Book Review

Henry Wadsworth Longfellow (1807–82)
Longfellow is to poetry what the barrel organ is to music.

> *Van Wyck Brooks*

Madonna (b 1958)
Sex (1992)—Mechanical soft porn, a listless cross between Henry Miller and Jackie Collins.

> *Ian Hamilton*

Sex (1992)—The book's erotic text is so dumb . . . that it makes the dialogue from an X-rated Ginger Lynn movie sound like vintage Anäis Nin. Sex is, forgive the expression, an anticlimax.

> Rolling Stone

Norman Mailer (b 1923)
If he has a taste for transcribing banalities, he also has a talent for it.

> New Republic

Harlot's Ghost (1991)—The last line of this immense book [1310 pages] reads "To Be Continued." The thought is enough to send a reader in search of a drink.

> *Peter S. Prescott*
> Newsweek

Harlot's Ghost (1991)—The author does come across as a punch-drunk writer trying to outbox all competition, real or imaginary.

> *John Simon*
> New York Times
> Book Review

Karl Marx (1818–83)
Das Kapital (1867)—The first volume of *Kapital* is badly written, ill put together, lacking in order, logic, and homogeneity of material.

> *Jacques Barzun*

The world would not be in such a snarl,
Had Marx been Groucho instead of Karl.

> *Irving Berlin*

M is for Marx
And clashing of the classes
And movement of masses
And massing of asses.

> *Cyril Connolly*

W. Somerset Maugham (1874–1965)
Of Human Bondage (1935)—Largely a record of sordid realism.

> The Athenaeum

Henry Miller (1891–1980)
Tropic of Cancer (1934)— . . . is without literary value.

> *Brigid Brophy*
> London *(1963)*

John Milton (1608–74)
Paradise Lost (1667)—I could never read ten lines together without stumbling at some Pedantry that tipped me at once out of Paradise, or even Hell, into the schoolroom, worse than either.

> *Edward Fitzgerald, letter*
> *(1876)*

Lycidas (1638)—The diction is harsh, the rhymes uncertain, and the numbers unpleasing. . . . Its form is that of a pastoral—easy, vulgar, and therefore disgusting.

> *Samuel Johnson*
> Lives of the English Poets
> *(1779)*

Andrew Morton (b 1953)
Diana: Her Private Story (1992)—Royal biographies
were pastel-tinted hagiographies . . . but *Diana* by
contrast, looked like a portrait painted by Edvard
Munch.

Julie Llewellyn-Smith

Diana: Her Private Story (1992)—Andrew More-Tons-
of-garbage.

Private Eye

Vladimir Nabokov (1899–1977)
Lolita (1959)—It is overwhelmingly nauseating, even
to an enlightened Freudian. It is a totally perverse
performance all round. I am most disturbed at the
thought that the writer has asked that this be published.
I can see no possible cause that could be served by its
publication now. I recommend that it be buried under a
stone for a thousand years.

Anonymous publisher (1955)

Mr. Nabokov is in the habit of introducing any job of
this kind which he undertakes by the announcement
that he is unique and incomparable, and that everybody
else who has attempted it is an oaf and ignoramus,
usually with the implication that he is also a low-class
person and a ridiculous personality.

Edmund Wilson

Friedrich Nietzsche (1844–1900)
He belongs, body and soul, to the flock of mangy
sheep.

Max Nordau
Degeneration

An agile but unintelligent and abnormal German,
possessed of the mania of grandeur.

Leo Tolstoy

Daniel Odier (b 1945)
Cannibal Kiss (1989)—*Cannibal Kiss* took me three
hours to read carefully, and I'm a slow reader;
unfortunately the book's anemic prose left me with the
impression that the novel hadn't taken much longer to
write.

William Mooney
American Book Review

George Orwell (1903–50)
1984 (1949)—George Orwell and his stupid book.

Isaac Asimov

Tall, pale, with his flaccid cheeks, large spatulate
fingers, and supercilious voice, he was one of those
boys who seem born old.

Cyril Connolly

Thomas Paine (1737–1809)
Common Sense (1776)—Shallow, violent, and scurrilous.

William E. H. Lecky (1882)

William Lyon Phelps
Happiness—It is second only to a rubber duck as the ideal bathtub companion. It may be held in the hand without causing muscular fatigue . . . and it may be read through before the water has cooled. And if it slips down the drainpipe, all right, it slips down the drainpipe.

Dorothy Parker
New Yorker *(1927)*

Edgar Allan Poe (1809–49)
A verbal poet merely; empty of thought, empty of sympathy, empty of love for any real thing . . . he was not human and manly.

John Burroughs
The Dial *(1893)*

Ezra Pound (1885–1972)
He was humane but not human.

e e cummings

He was a crackpot.

Nigel Frith

He has no real creative theme. His versification and his proses are servants to willful ideas and platform vehemences. His moral attitudes and absolutisms are bullying assertions, and have the uncreative blatancy of one whose Social Credit consorts naturally with Fascism and anti-Semitism.

> *F. R. Leavis*

Marcel Proust (1871–1922)
A society creep and sniveling hermit.

> *Andrew Hope (1990)*

Marcel Proust is to life what an empty orchestra pit is to music.

> *John Naughton (1991)*

Remembrance of Things Past (1928)—So full of dignitaries, so devoid of dignity.

> Saturday Review of
> Literature

Mario Puzo (b 1920)
The Last Don (1997)—*Godfather* minestrone, with bits from parts 1, 2, and 3 all tossed into a lukewarm pot.

> Entertainment Weekly

J. Danforth Quayle (b 1947)

Standing Firm (1994)—The year's most unawaited book.

> Dave Shiplett

Sally Quinn (b 1941)

She is a water bug on the surface of life.

> *Gloria Steinem (1992)*

James Redfield

The Tenth Insight (1996)—Feel-good metaphysical goop.

> Entertainment Weekly

Anne Rice (b 1941)

Servant of the Bones (1996), *featuring an ancient spirit called Azriel*—"Perhaps the story is chaos," Azriel muses at one point. Couldn't describe it better ourselves.

> Entertainment Weekly

Memnoch the Devil: The Vampire Chronicles (1995)—A narrative that's oddly arid, despite a few token episodes of bloodsucking.

> *Wendy Scott*
> New York Times
> Book Review

Memnoch the Devil: The Vampire Chronicles (1995)—
Rice routinely fills her novels with tedious
pseudotheology, but she really goes overboard here.
. . . This clumsily told tale manages to be both
ludicrous and offensive.

> *Donna Seaman*
> Booklist

Philip Roth (b 1933)
His specialty is the varnished truth.

> *Paul Gray*
> Miami Herald *(1987)*

J. D. Salinger (b 1919)
The greatest mind ever to stay in prep school.

> *Norman Mailer*

George Sand (1804–76)
She has the habit of speaking and writing concerning
chastity in such terms that makes the very word
become impure.

> *Philip Hale*

George Santayana (1863–1952)
The perfection of rottenness.

> *William James*

William Saroyan (1908–81)

The Human Condition (1943)—An excessively simple and very, very sentimental little concoction.

Times Literary Supplement
(London)

(Sir) Walter Scott (1771–1832)

Kenilworth—A wonderful human being and a monumentally boring writer. I would love to have dined with him but I cannot bring myself to read *Kenilworth*.

Richard Huggett
The Wit of Publishing
(1986)

He sets the world in love with dreams and phantoms; with decayed and swinish forms of religion; with decayed and degraded systems of government; with the silliness and emptiness, sham gauds, and sham chivalries of a brainless and worthless long-vanished society. He did measureless harm; more real and lasting harm, perhaps, than any other individual that ever wrote.

Mark Twain

Linda Scottoline

Legal Tender (1996)—Anybody who wants to argue that the legal-thriller fad is running out of gas could use *Legal Tender* as Exhibit A.

Gene Lyons
Entertainment Weekly

William Shakespeare (1564–1616)
The sonnets beginning CXXVII to his mistress are
worse than a puzzle-peg. They are abominably harsh,
obscure, and worthless. . . . Their chief faults—and
heavy ones they are—are sameness, tediousness,
quaintness, and elaborate obscurity.

William Wordsworth

George Bernard Shaw (1856–1950)
The Adventures of a Black Girl in Her Search for God
(1932)—A profoundly stupid book and a profoundly
ignorant book.

Archbishop of York (1934)

Gail Sheehy (b 1937)
New Passages (1995)—The author's role is social
director aboard a lifeboat.

Janet Maslin
New York Times

Percy Bysshe Shelley (1792–1822)
The school to which he belonged, or rather which he
established, can never become popular.

Philadelphia Monthly *(1828)*

Shelley should not be read, but inhaled through a gas
pipe.

Lionel Trilling

Gertrude Stein (1874–1946)

The words employed by Gertrude Stein may be said to resemble poetry because poetry consists of words, and so does her crazy clatter.

> Boston Evening Transcript
> *(1927)*

I know of no one except Miss Stein who can roll out this completely nonresistant prose, prose that puts you at once in a condition resembling the early stages of grippe—the eyes and legs heavy, the top of the skull wandering around in an uncertain and independent manner, the heart ponderously, tirelessly beating.

> *Clifton Fadiman*

"Sacred Emily"
The fault I'm sure is solely mine,
But I cannot root for Gertrude Stein.
For Gertrude Stein I cannot root;
I cannot blow a single toot. . . .

> *Ogden Nash*

In her last days, she resembled a spoiled pear.

> *Gore Vidal*

Robert Louis Stevenson (1850–94)

A Presbyterian pirate.

> *Doris Dalglish*

Jacqueline Susann (1926–74)
She looks like a truck driver in drag.

Truman Capote

Jonathan Swift (1667–1745)
Gulliver's Travels (1726)—Evidence of a diseased mind
and lacerated heart.

John Dunlop
The History of Fiction
(1814)

Donna Tartt (b 1964)
The Secret History (1992)—Naive and poised by turns
. . . like a B movie written by a schoolgirl.

Kathy O'Shaughnessy
Vogue

The Secret History (1992)—We've seen it all before—
the money, the Hollywood deals, the author profiles.
As for this new girl Donna Tartt, even her name
sounds like a confection cooked up by marketing.

Harvey Porlock
The Times *of London*

Lou Tellegen
Women Have Been Kind—The book . . . has all the
elegance of a quirked little finger and all the glitter of
a new pair of rubber gloves.

Dorothy Parker
New Yorker *(1927)*

Alfred, Lord Tennyson (1809–92)
"The Charge of the Light Brigade" (1854)—If you see Tennyson, ask him how he came to write all that rot about Balaclava.

> Lord Cardigan
> (British commander) (1854)

A dirty man with opium-glazed eyes and rat-taily hair.

> Lady Frederick Cavendish

Alfred Lawn Tennyson.

> James Joyce

Margaret Thatcher (b 1925)
The Downing Street Years (autobiography) (1993)—It sets standards of self-regard hitherto unknown. . . . She is continually giving herself standing ovations.

> Nigel Lawson

Dylan Thomas (1914–53)
Thomas was an outstandingly unpleasant man, one who cheated and stole from his friends and peed on their carpets.

> Kingsley Amis

He was cartilaginous, out of humanity, the Disembodied
Gland, which was my coinage; Ditch, which was
Norman Cameron's; the Ugly Suckling, which was
Bernard Spencer's, indicating a willful and at times nasty
babyishness.

Geoffrey Grigson

James Thurber (1894–1961)
On Thurber's cartoon dogs—Stop running those dogs on
my page. I wouldn't have them peeing on my cheapest
rug.

William Randolph Hearst

A tall, thin, spectacled man with the face of a harassed
rat.

Russell Maloney

Alice B. Toklas (1877–1967)
She was incredibly ugly, uglier than almost anyone I
had ever met. A thin, withered creature, she sat
hunched in her chair, in her heavy tweed suit and her
thick lisle stockings, impregnable and indifferent. She
had a huge nose, a dark mustache, and her dark-dyed
hair was combed into absurd bangs over her forehead.

Otto Friedrich

J. R. R. Tolkien (1892–1973)
On reading Tolkien's latest manuscript—Oh, f***! Not
another elf!

Hugo Dyson

His appeal is to readers with a lifelong appetite for juvenile trash.

Edmund Wilson

Leo Tolstoy (1828–1910)
War and Peace (1869)—I haven't read *War and Peace* but that's a man's book, anyway.

Kaye Gibbons (1990)

Anna Karenina (1877)—Sentimental rubbish. . . . Show me one page that contains an idea.

Odessa Courier

War and Peace (1869)—A stodgy pudding of events mixed by a loveless, zestless, boring egotist who wanted to write a big book.

Rebecca West

Garry Trudeau (b 1948)
On his Doonesbury *comic strip*—He speaks for a bunch of Chardonnay-sipping elitists.

George Bush
Life *(1995)*

[*Trudeau had earlier said*:
Criticizing a political satirist for being unfair is like criticizing a nose guard for being physical.
Newsweek (1990)]

Ivana Trump (b 1949)
Perhaps the single greatest creation of the idiot
culture, a tabloid artifact if ever there was one.

> *Carl Bernstein*
> New Republic

For Love Alone (1992)—Set down next to say, Ivana
Trump, Jack Higgins suddenly looks like a master of
the pithy phrase.

> Private Eye

Mark Twain (Samuel Langhorne Clemens)
(1835–1910)
The Adventures of Huckleberry Finn (1884)—The
adolescent dream goes on, lulling the reader into an
immature climate where goodness somehow triumphs
and yet every tribute is paid to the abstract concept of
boyishness. It is a vision that can be achieved only by
that ruthless dishonesty which is the birthright of
every sentimentalist.

> *Brophy, Levey, and Osborne*
> 50 Works of Literature We
> Could Do Without *(1967)*

He had a vanity that makes Donald Trump look like a
nun.

> *Garrison Keillor (1990)*

A hundred years from now it is very likely that "The Jumping Frog" alone will be remembered.

> *Harry T. Peck*
> The Bookman *(1901)*

The Adventures of Huckleberry Finn (1884)—A gross trifling with every fine feeling. . . . Mr. Clemens has no reliable sense of propriety.

> Springfield Republican

John Updike (b 1932)

Rabbit Run (1960)—The author fails to convince us that his puppets are interesting in themselves or that their plight has implications that transcend their narrow world.

> *Milton Crane*
> Chicago Tribune

Rabbit at Rest (1990)—Had Updike done more dramatizing and less editorializing, he might have created a series that would outlive its period. But the books bog down in opinion, and opinion is a poor substitute for appetite.

> *James Wolcott*

Gore Vidal (b 1925)

A tart . . . an embittered man.

> *Charlton Heston*
> Esquire *(1997)*

Robert James Waller (b 1939)
The Bridges of Madison County—It's the end of the
world as we know it. It's the big lie. It's everything
bad in literature and in life.

Jacquelyn Mitchard (1996)

Evelyn Waugh (1903–66)
His style has the desperate jauntiness of an orchestra
fiddling away for dear life on a sinking ship.

Edmund Wilson

Noah Webster (1758–1843)
It is a melancholy proof of the amount of mischief
one man of learning can do to society that Webster's
system of orthography is adopted and propagated.

William Cullen Bryant

H. G. Wells (1866–1946)
He sold his birthright for a pot of message.

Anonymous

An anti-Semitic misogynist obsessed with the creation
of a racially pure master race.

Michael Coren (1992)

Walt Whitman (1819–91)

Leaves of Grass (1855)—The title is eclipsed in the
pages of this heterogeneous mess of bombast, egotism,
vulgarity, and nonsense. The author should be kicked
from all decent society as below the level of a brute—
it seems he must be some escaped lunatic, raving in
pitiable delirium.

Boston Intelligencer *(1856)*

He is the laureate of the empty deep incomprehensible.

Cincinnati Commercial
(1860)

Leaves of Grass (1855)—An auctioneer's inventory of a
warehouse . . . a singular blend of the *Bhagavad Gita*
and the *New York Tribune*.

Ralph Waldo Emerson

Whitman laid end to end words never seen in each
other's company before outside of a dictionary.

David Lodge

Leaves of Grass (1855)—The chief question raised by
Leaves of Grass is whether anybody—even a poet—
ought to take off his trousers in the market-place.

New York Tribune *(1881)*

The poetry of barbarism.

George Santayana (1900)

Whitman, like a large shaggy dog, just unchained,
scouring the beaches of the world baying at the moon.

Robert Louis Stevenson
Familiar Studies *(1882)*

Oscar Wilde (1854–1900)
The Picture of Dorian Gray (1891)—Unmanly,
sickening, vicious, and tedious.

The Athenaeum

Sloan Wilson (b 1920) **and Herman Wouk** (b 1915)
If the Man in the Grey Flannel Suit married Marjorie
Morningstar on my front porch at high noon, I
wouldn't bother to go to the wedding.

Nelson Algren

Kathleen Winsor (b 1919)
On the Massachusetts Superior Court ruling that Forever
Amber *could be put on sale*—While conducive to sleep,
it is not conducive to a desire to sleep with a member
of the opposite sex.

Judge Frank J. Donahue

Naomi Wolf (b 1962)
She's a parent-pleasing, teacher-pleasing little kiss-ass.

Camille Paglia

Tom Wolfe (b 1931)

The nonchalant master of the neon-piped sentence.

Hugh Kenner

Virginia Woolf (1882–1941)

What a monster of egotism she was!

Louise Bogan

The Waves (1931)—This chamber music, this closet fiction, is executed behind too firmly closed windows. . . . The book is dull.

H. C. Harwood
Saturday Review of
Literature

To the Lighthouse (1927)—Her work is poetry; it must be judged as poetry, and all the weaknesses of poetry are inherent in it.

New York Evening Post

She had been a peculiar kind of snob without really belonging to a social group with whom to be snobbish.

Edmund Wilson

William Wordsworth (1770–1850)

An old half-witted sheep.

J. K. Stephen

William Butler Yeats (1865–1939)
Yeats is second-rate, but the rest are fourth-rate.

Nigel Frith

The Wind Among the Reeds (1899)—Neither rhyme nor reason do I find in one single page. . . . These books are to me absolutely empty and void.

John Morley (1900)

Yevgeny Yevtushenko (b 1933)
Don't Die Before You're Dead (1995)—If this tome had been written by a Bulgarian, no American publisher would have touched it. The exaggerated appetite for things Russian that developed during the cold war still allows many Russians to make careers in this country for no good reason.

Ewa M. Thompson
America

8

NEWSPAPERS AND MAGAZINES

From the American newspapers, you'd think America was populated by naked women and cinema stars.

Nancy Astor (1957)

America is a country of inventors, and the greatest of inventors are the newspaper men.

Alexander Graham Bell (1917)

The fallacy of the press is still rampant in this decaying and foolish world.

Noël Coward
Pomp and Circumstance

The press can be best compared to hemorrhoids.

Gareth Davies

That ephemeral sheet of paper, the newspaper, is the natural enemy of the book, as the whore is of the decent woman.

> *Edmond and Jules*
> *De Goncourt*
> Journal *(1858)*

The relationship between truth and a newspaper is like the relationship between the color green and the number seven. Occasionally you will see the number seven written in green, but you learn not to expect this.

> *Garrison Keillor*

Once a newspaper touches a story, the facts are lost forever, even to the protagonists.

> *Norman Mailer*
> Esquire *(1960)*

The press should take a lesson from the under-tens. It might learn something.

> *John McEnroe (1984)*

The British newspapers are edited by Kitty Kelley. They are only interested in character assassination.

> *Rudolf Nureyev (1991)*

The newspaper and magazine business is an intellectual brothel from which there is no escape.

> *Leo Tolstoy*

PUBLICATIONS

Cosmopolitan
The fashion pages of magazines such as *Cosmopolitan* now seem to specialize in telling the career girl what to wear to charm the particular wrong type of man who reads *Playboy*, while the editorial pages tell her how to cope with the resulting psychic damage.

> *Alison Lurie*
> The Language of Clothes
> *(1981)*

Counterfeit
If you continue to publish slanderous pieces about me, I shall feel compelled to cancel my subscription.

> *Groucho Marx, letter*

New Yorker
It seems to do with ink and paper what morticians do with formaldehyde.

> *Paul Theroux*
> New York Times *(1990)*

Pungent and artless . . . what one would call low-falutin'.

> *Kenneth Tynan*

New York Newsday
A tabloid in a tutu.

> *Anonymous*

New York Post
When she refused to take advertising space in the paper—
Your readers are my shoplifters.

> *Betsy Bloomingdale,*
> *letter to Rupert Murdoch*
> *(1986)*

I enjoy the *Post* as a comic book.

> *Mort Zuckerman*
> New York *(1994)*

New York Times
Viewing with dismay the conditions in somebody else's
backyard is the specialty of the *New York Times.*

> *John Crosby*

It reads like it was edited by two elderly sociologists,
one of whom has been dead for many years.

> *Garrison Keillor (1990)*

Regina (Canada) Leader
The MisLeader.

> *Nickname (circa 1923)*

Sports Illustrated
If there is one specific time during the year that my spirits and coincidentally my bosoms are at their lowest, it is the day the *Sports Illustrated* swimsuit issue comes out. By the way, wearing swimsuits is a sport like ketchup is a vegetable.

> *Rita Rudner*
> Naked Beneath My Clothes
> *(1992)*

The Times *of London*
On The Times *reporting of Home Rule in Ireland—The* Times is speechless and takes three columns to express its speechlessness.

> *Winston Churchill (1908)*

The Turnabout.

> *Nickname*

Toronto Globe
A literary despotism which struck without mercy.

> *Goldwyn Smith (1883)*

Toronto Star
King Street Pravda.

> *Anonymous (circa 1930)*

Town & Country
Vanity Fair is for the thinking rich, and *Town & Country* is for the stinking rich.

Tina Brown

USA Today
It is like a bus schedule for people who can't get to the depot . . . doesn't give you much but tells you when the bus is leaving.

Peter Andrews
American Heritage *(1994)*

Variety
On its trademark showbiz language—I read Shakespeare very well. *Variety* I still cannot read.

Walter Winchell

Village Voice
A basically unreadable rag of pseudoradical pretension.

Wilda Williams
Library Journal

Wall Street Journal
The *Wall Street Journal* criticizing my wife for making money is like *Field & Stream* criticizing people for catching fish.

Bill Clinton *(1994)*

EDITORS AND PUBLISHERS

If there is anything tougher than a sports editor, I should not like to meet it.

Earl of Arran (1962)

The modern editor of a paper does not want facts. The editor wants novelty. He would prefer a novelty that is not a fact to a fact that is not a novelty.

William Randolph Hearst
(circa 1930s)

Perhaps an editor might divide his paper into four chapters; heading the first, Truths; the second, Probabilities; the third, Possibilities; and the fourth, Lies.

Thomas Jefferson

Anonymous

I can but wonder what will become of the editor of the *Los Angeles Times* when the breath leaves his feculent body and death stops the rattling of his abortive brain. He cannot be buried in the sea lest he poison the fishes. He cannot be suspended in mid-air, like Mahomet's coffin, lest the circling worlds, in their endeavor to avoid contamination, crash together, wreck the universe, and bring about the return of chaos and Old Night. The damn scoundrel is a white elephant on the hands of the Deity, and I have some curiosity to know what He will do with him.

W. C. Brann

Ben Bradlee, editor of the *Washington Post*
(b 1921)
Preppy, tweedier-than-thou arrogance.

Anonymous

William F. Buckley, Jr., editor of *New Republic*
(b 1925)
It's great to be with Bill Buckley, because you don't have to think. He takes a position and you automatically take the opposite and you know you're right.

John Kenneth Galbraith

Horace Greeley, editor of *New York Tribune* (1811–72)

The repentant male Magdalen of New York journalism.

James G. Bennett, Sr.

Poor Greeley, a nincompoop without genius.

William J. Grayson

Frank Harris, editor of *Vanity Fair* (1856–1931)

Can there ever have been, since St. Paul, such a pompous, conceited, opinionated, patronizing ass? Patronizing Ruskin, Carlyle, Whitman, Wilde, and the Prince of Wales; patronizing the Parthenon or the whole continent of North America; patronizing the arts, patronizing philosophy, patronizing God. Prose stodgy and repetitious; moralizing at once trite and windy; and as for the celebrated sex, orgasms going off as noisily and monotonously as a twenty-one gun salute—to Frank Harris, of course.

Simon Raven

William Randolph Hearst, publisher of the *New York Journal* and the *San Francisco Examiner* (1863–1951)

The world's worst son of a bitch.

Dorothy Parker

Hugh Hefner, publisher of *Playboy* (b 1926)
His philosophy would not impress anyone with as
much knowledge of the subject as can be gained by
catching sight of a copy of a popular philosophical
digest in a bookcase on the other side of a fairly large
room.

Anonymous

If he has done nothing else for American culture, he
has given it two of the great lies of the twentieth
century: "I buy it for the fiction" and "I buy it for the
interviews."

Nora Ephron

On the TV documentary "The World of Hugh
Hefner"—Mocking Hugh Hefner is easy to do, and in
my mind, should be made easier.

Clive James (1974)

Henry Luce, publisher of *Time, Fortune,* and *Life*
(1898–1967)
His exterior conceals the most arrogant conceit and
the most ruthlessly hard-boiled self-assurance it has
ever been my privilege to come up against.

Cyrus Sulzberger

H. L. Mencken, editor of *The Smart Set*

(1880–1956)

The world's greatest alphabetical mountebank, perpetually suffering from logomachitis, or acute inflammation of the stylus. If all he writes is true, he is a very sick man.

Chicago Step-Ladder

If he and the pusillanimous curs who are backing him are right, Judas Iscariot should be sainted, and an American shrine should be erected to the memory of Benedict Arnold.

L. L. Hayden

Mr. Mencken's prose sounds like large stones being thrown into a dump-cart.

Robert Littell

Mr. Mencken did not degenerate from an ape, but an ass. And in the process of "revolution" the tail was eliminated, the ears became shorter, and the hind parts smaller; but the ability to bray was increased, intensified, amplified, and otherwise assified about one million times.

J. B. Tedder

**Rupert Murdoch, publisher of the *New York Post*
and *The Times* of London** (b 1933)
The man's charm is lethal. One minute he's swimming
along with a smile, then snap! There's blood in the
water. Your head's gone.

John Barry

He believes that people crave rubbish and that he has
the right to grow rich providing it.

Simon Hoggart (1992)

The enemy in question is that drivel-merchant, global
huckster, and so-to-speak media psychopath.

Dennis Potter (1993)

On his Australian roots—"The Dirty Digger."

Private Eye

No self-respecting dead fish would want to be wrapped
in a Murdoch newspaper, let alone work for it.

George Royko (1986)

Rupert Murdoch has made a fortune from selling
excrement and, in the process, has debauched our
culture and corrupted our youths, producing a
generation of lager louts, sex maniacs, and morons.

Francis Wheen
Literary Review

Harrison Gray Otis,
publisher of the *Los Angeles Times* (1837–1917)
In the city of San Francisco we have drunk to the
very dregs of infamy; we have had vile officials, we
have had rotten newspapers. But we have nothing so
vile, nothing so low, nothing so debased, nothing so
infamous in San Francisco as Harrison Gray Otis. He
sits there in senile dementia, with gangrened heart and
rotting brain, grimacing at every reform, chatting
impotently at all things that are decent, frothing,
fuming, violently gibbering, going down to his grave
in snarling infamy.

Hiram Johnson

Harold Ross, editor of the *New Yorker* (1892–1951)
At first view, oddly disappointing. Even in dinner
jacket he looked loosely informal, like a carelessly
carried umbrella.

James Thurber (1927)

Ross, a man who knew nothing and had contempt for
everything he didn't understand, which was practically
everything.

Alexander Woollcott

JOURNALISTS

Journalism could be described as turning one's enemies into money.

Craig Brown (1990)

Skin a hard-boiled journalist and you find a thwarted idealist.

Russell Green

Newspapermen: the hand of God reaching down into the mire couldn't elevate one of them to the depths of degradation—not by a million miles.

Ben Hecht
Nothing Sacred *(1937)*

Reporters are puppets. They simply respond to the pull of the most powerful strings.

Lyndon B. Johnson

The lowest depth to which people can sink before God is defined by the word *journalist*. If I were a father and had a daughter who was seduced I should despair over her; I would hope for her salvation. But if I had a son who became a journalist and continued to be one for five years, I would give him up.

Søren Kierkegaard

On gossip columnists—I've always felt those articles somehow reveal more about the writer than they do about me.

> Marilyn Monroe

Women journalists are harlots. Harlots of the day, not the night.

> James Pickles (1990)

Journalists belong in the gutter because that is where the ruling classes throw their guilty secrets.

> Gerald Priestland (1988)

American female hacks tend to psychoanalyze everything, including household pets.

> "Taki"
> The Spectator (1992)

Journalism is a low trade and a habit worse than heroin, a strange seedy world full of misfits and drunkards and failures. A group photo of the Top Ten journalists in America on any given day would be a monument to human ugliness.

> Hunter S. Thompson (1988)

The American president reigns for four years, and journalists govern for ever and ever.

> Oscar Wilde (1891)

There is much to be said in favor of modern journalism. By giving us the opinions of the uneducated, it keeps us in touch with the ignorance of the community.

Oscar Wilde
Intentions *(1891)*

A journalist makes up his lies
And takes you by the throat.

William Butler Yeats
"The Old Stone Cross"
(1938)

Anonymous American columnist
She's one great stampede from nose to navel.

Noël Coward

Rona Barrett
She doesn't need a steak knife. Rona cuts her food with her tongue.

Johnny Carson

Carl Bernstein, *Washington Post* (b 1944)
Carl liked the midnight glitter, while Bob [Woodward] loved the midnight oil.

Ben Bradlee

Rowland Evans and Robert Novak, "Inside Report" columnists

They ought to be called "Errors and No Facts."

Thomas P. "Tip" O'Neill

Joyce Haber

They should give Haber open-heart surgery . . . and go in through the feet.

Julie Andrews

Philip Hodson

He thinks he's writing for the *Journal of Psychology* . . . His column is going down like a cup of cold sick.

Anonymous

Hedda Hopper (1890–1966)

Timid? As timid as a buzzsaw.

George Ells

Listen, dearie. I was at the top when you were a has-been practicing to be a never-was.

Louella Parsons (1985)

Ralph Ingersoll

He was as persistent as snow in Alaska.

Erskine Caldwell

He had awesome hypochondria . . . twelve yards of quivering mucous membrane.

Robert T. Elson
Time Inc. *(1968)*

Dorothy Kilgallen (1913–65)
She must use Novocain lipstick.

Jack Paar

Walter Lippmann (1899–1974)
I am going to sit on this porch for two years, doze, and think. And then one day I will get up and get Walter Lippmann.

Lyndon B. Johnson

Norman Mailer (b 1923)
The patron saint of bad journalism.

Gore Vidal

Suzanne Moore
A feminist of the younger school . . . f***-me shoes and three fat inches of cleavage . . . so much lipstick must rot the brain.

Germaine Greer (1995)

Paparazzi

Those long, penetrating lenses . . . cause us to wear
T-shirts when we go swimming . . . because we don't
want to be analyzed by the doctors from the *New York
Times*.

George Bush (1988)

*After a press photographer asked his name at the first night
of his* Pacific 1860 (1946)—I recommend you to *Who's
Who*—and Hell.

Noël Coward

When I see them around all the time, it is like being
raped.

Princess Diana (1995)

Louella Parsons

Hearst's Hollywood stooge.

Joel Faith

You turn the whole nation into a sewing circle
without too much needle.

Bob Hope

She interpreted denials as the great horned owl
interprets the squeaking of distant mice.

Paul O'Neil
Life (1965)

Drew Pearson (1897–1969)

An unprincipled, degenerate liar . . . a man who has been able to sugarcoat his wares so well that he has been able to fool vast numbers of people with his fake piety and false loyalty.

Joseph McCarthy (senator)

I wish I was still in Chicago so I could have that son of a bitch rubbed out.

Eleanor Medill Patterson

Everyone makes mistakes, but the SOB makes a racket, a business, a mint of money, writing fiction in the guise of news reporting.

Walter Winchell

Hannen Swaffer

Whenever I see his fingernails, I thank God I don't have to look at his feet.

Athene Seyler

Walter Winchell (1897–1972)

He was truly a fourteen-carat son of a bitch, no doubt about it. He looked like a cross between a weasel and a jackal, and he was indeed a bit of both.

John Crosby

9
POLITICS

The trouble with some of the big guns in politics is
that they are of small caliber and are big bores.

Anonymous

I was not meant for the spotlight of public life in
Washington. Here running people down is considered
sport.

Vincent W. Foster, Jr.,
suicide letter (1993)

The word *politics* is derived from the word *poly,*
meaning *many,* and the word *ticks,* meaning
bloodsucking parasites.

Larry Hardiman

Conferences at the top level are always courteous.
Name-calling is left to the foreign ministers.

W. Averell Harriman (1955)

A dilemma is a politician trying to save both of his
faces at once.

John A. Lincoln

Render any politician down and there's enough fat to
fry an egg.

*Terence "Spike" Milligan
(1968)*

In political discussion, heat is in inverse proportion to
knowledge.

J. G. Minchin

A man should always be drunk when he talks of
politics . . . it's the only way in which to make them
important.

Sean O'Casey
The Shadow of a Gunman

In politics, people give you what they think you
deserve, and deny you what you think you want.

Cecil Parkinson (1990)

POLITICIANS

On retiring as secretary of state—I will have to seek what is happily known as gainful employment, which I am glad to say does not describe holding public office.

Dean Acheson (1962)

I always say gridlock's a good thing. . . . That's what the founding fathers had in mind when they created the Senate.

Bob Dole (1993)

The outcome of twenty-five years of Republican rule (Jimmy Carter was a mere blip in 1976) is that Americans have learned to hate themselves, like children of repressive, conformist families.

Cynthia Heimel (1992)

If God had meant us to vote, he'd have given us candidates.

Ice-T (1993)

The Republican convention started this past weekend, so don't forget to turn your clocks back four hundred years.

Jay Leno (1996)

On the 1960 Democratic National Convention—A man of taste, arrived from Mars, would take one look at the convention floor and leave forever, convinced he had seen one of the drearier squats of Hell.

Norman Mailer

Congress: these, for the most part, illiterate hacks whose fancy vests are spotted with gravy and whose speeches, hypocritical, unctuous, and slovenly, are spotted also with the gravy of political patronage.

Mary McCarthy
On the Contrary *(1962)*

The American political system is like fast food: mushy, insipid, made out of disgusting parts of things—and everybody wants some.

P. J. O'Rourke
Parliament of Whores *(1991)*

Politicians—a number of anxious dwarfs trying to grill a whale.

J. B. Priestley
Outcries and Asides *(1974)*

Politicians are people who, when they see the light at the end of the tunnel, order more tunnel.

Sir John Quinton
Money *(1989)*

On her male colleagues in Congress—We have got an
awful lot of members who don't understand that *harass*
is one word, not two.

> Pat Schroeder *(1996)*

The effectiveness of a politician varies in inverse
proportion to his commitment to a principle.

> Sam Shaffer
> Newsweek *(1971)*

The hatred Americans have for their own government
is pathological. At one level it is simply thwarted
greed: since our religion is making a buck, giving a
part of that back to any government is an act against
nature.

> Gore Vidal

History is not going to be kind to liberals. With their
mindless programs, they've managed to do to Black
Americans what slavery, Reconstruction, and rank
racism found impossible: destroy their family and work
ethic.

> Walter Williams

Dean Acheson (1893–1971)

I hope Mr. Acheson will write a book explaining how
he persuaded himself to believe that a government
could be conducted without the support of the people.

> Walter Lippmann

Spiro Agnew (1918–96)

Agnew reminds me of the kind of guy who would make a crank call to the Russians on the hot line.

Dick Gregory

Mr. Agnew preached the old-fashioned values and practiced old-fashioned vices.

Eric Sevareid

A medicine man whose remedies would put an end to the patient as well as the problem.

Tom Wicker

Aldrich H. Ames

There are some important differences between Benedict Arnold and Ames—all in Arnold's favor.

R. James Woolsey (1994)

Thomas H. Benton (1792–1858)

The greatest of all humbugs, and could make more out of nothing than any other man in the world. He ought to have gone about all his life with quack doctors and written puffs for their medicines. Had he done so, he might have made a fortune.

John C. Calhoun

William Jennings Bryan (1860–1925)
A mouthing, slobbering demagogue whose patriotism
is all jawbone.

Thomas Dixon (1896)

We put him to school and he wound up stealing the
schoolbooks.

Ignatius Donnelly

A wretched, rattle-pated boy, posing in vanity and
mouthing resounding rottenness.

New York Tribune *(1896)*

Aaron Burr (1756–1836)
Toast at the time of Burr's trial—May his treachery to
his country exalt him to the scaffold, and hemp be his
escort to the republic of dust and ashes.

Anonymous

He is in every sense a profligate; a voluptuary in the
extreme, with uncommon habits of expense. He is
artful and intriguing to an inconceivable degree. As
unprincipled and dangerous a man as any country can
boast—as true a Catiline as ever met in midnight
conclave.

*Alexander Hamilton, letter
(1800)*

Henry Clay (1777–1852)
He is half-educated. His morals, public or private, are loose.

John Quincy Adams

He is a bad man, an imposter, a creator of wicked schemes.

John C. Calhoun

He is certainly the basest, meanest scoundrel that ever disgraced the image of God, nothing too mean or too low for him to condescend.

Andrew Jackson

Hillary Clinton (b 1947)
On why the First Lady refused to bare her butt in a magazine spread—They don't have a page that broad.

Gennifer Flowers (1992)

That smiling barracuda.

National Review *(1993)*

John Connally (1917–95)
John ain't been worth a damn since he started wearing three-hundred-dollar suits.

Lyndon B. Johnson

Alfonse M. D'Amato (b 1937)

If hypocrisy were an Olympic event, Al would win gold, silver, and bronze.

Mark Green (1995)

Eugene Debs (1855–1926)

Debs has a face that looks like a death's head. . . . As the arch-Red talked, he was bent at the hips like an old man, his eerie face peering up and out at the crowd like a necromancer leading a charm.

Los Angeles Times *(1908)*

Thomas E. Dewey (1902–71)

He's the only man able to walk under a bed without hitting his head.

Walter Winchell

Bob Dole (b 1923)

When he does smile, he looks as if he's just evicted a widow.

Mike Royko (1988)

Stephen Douglas (1813–61)

A brutal vulgar man without delicacy or scholarship . . . looks as if he needed clean linen and should be put under a shower head.

Charles Sumner

Michael Dukakis (b 1933)
He's the stealth candidate. His campaign jets from
place to place, but no issues show up on the radar
screen.

George Bush

Radiating all the studly presidential command of
Rocket J. Squirrel.

Owen Gleiberman
Entertainment Weekly *(1997)*

Pinchgut Mickey.

P. J. O'Rourke
Parliament of Whores *(1991)*

David Duke (b 1951)
Racism in a business suit.

Edward M. Kennedy (1991)

John Foster Dulles (1888–1959)
Mr. Dulles' moral universe makes everything quite
clear, too clear—self-righteousness is the inevitable
fruit of simple moral judgments.

Reinhold Niebuhr

A cold, arrogant, and ruthless man who has been
exhausting himself running around the world because
he really trusts no one.

Adlai Stevenson

Dulles is a man of wily and subtle mind. It is difficult to believe that behind his unctuous manner he does not take a cynical amusement in his own monstrous pomposities.

I. F. Stone

William Fulbright (b 1905)
You know you're milking a cow and you have all that foamy white milk in the bucket and you're just about through when all of a sudden the cow swishes her tail through a pile of manure and splashes it into that foamy white milk? Well, that's William Fulbright.

Lyndon B. Johnson (1967)

John Wesley Gaines
John Wesley Gaines!
John Wesley Gaines!
Thou monumental mass of brains!
Come in, John Wesley, 'fore it rains.

Anonymous

John Glenn (b 1921)
Senator Glenn couldn't electrify a fish tank if he threw a toaster in it.

Dave Barry

Samuel Gompers (1850–1924)

Wholly un-American in appearance: short, with large eyes, dark complexion, heavy-lined face, and hair slightly curly, but looking moth-eaten—he was impressive. As I sat in the audience, I wrote the name "Marat" on a slip of paper and handed it to my companion. He nodded.

Walter G. Merrit
Destination Unknown *(1951)*

Al Gore (b 1948)

Al Gore is like the fat boy in the schoolyard. Tormenting him is so much fun nobody can resist. . . . a natural-born victim.

Russell Baker
New York Times *(1997)*

When he speaks, he often sounds like a schoolteacher talking to a second-grade class.

Russell Baker
New York Times *(1997)*

Q: How can you tell Al Gore from his secret service agents?
A: He's the stiff one!

*Republican campaign joke
(1992)*

Hear Al Gore address the nation in verbal slo-mo, as if the entire populace labored under a grave learning disability.

> *Frank Rich*
> New York Times *(1996)*

John Hancock (1737–93)

A man without head and without heart . . . the mere shadow of a man—and yet Governor of old Massachusetts.

> *John Adams*

W. Averell Harriman (1891–1986)

He's thin, boys. He's thin as piss on a hot rock.

> *William E. Jenner*

Abbie Hoffman (1936–89)

He had a charisma that must have come out of an immaculate conception between Fidel Castro and Groucho Marx. They went into his soul and he came out looking like an ethnic milkshake: Jewish revolutionary, Puerto Rican lord, Italian street kid, Black Panther with the old Afro haircut, even a glint of Irish gunman in the mad, green eyes.

> *Norman Mailer (1989)*

Hubert H. Humphrey

Any political party that can't cough up anything better
than a treacherous, brain-damaged old vulture like
Hubert Humphrey deserves every beating it gets. They
don't hardly make 'em like Hubert any more—but just
to be on the safe side, he should be castrated anyway.

Hunter S. Thompson (1973)

Jesse Jackson

The hustler from Chicago.

George Bush (1988)

Have you ever noticed how all newspaper composite
pictures of wanted criminals resemble Jesse Jackson?

Rush Limbaugh
Newsday *(1990)*

Hamilton Jordan

He is a son of a bitch. The House Speaker is something
you bought at Radio Shack. I prefer to call him
Hannibal Jerken.

Thomas P. "Tip" O'Neill

Jack Kemp

Doctors in California have discovered that football
players who receive too many blows to the head can
become brain damaged and this can lead to poor
decision making later in life. That's why Kemp decided
to go with Dole.

Jay Leno (1996)

The Kennedy Family
There's never a dearth of reasons to shoot a Kennedy.

> *Don DeLillo*
> Libra *(1988)*

The Kennedys are like the dinosaurs in *The Lost World:* they have big teeth, breed like crazy, and wherever they go, women are running and screaming.

> *Jay Leno*
> *"The Tonight Show" (1997)*

People call them the American Royal Family. Unfortunately, they may be right.

> *Jim Mullen*
> Entertainment Weekly *(1997)*

Edward Kennedy (b 1932)
He couldn't get a whore across a bridge.

> *Attributed to Bill Clinton*

One of the prominent operators chosen by the hidden Forces that are hurling the countries of Western Europe towards the Animal Farm world willed by Lenin. This Force of Darkness has already brought the world near to the point of no return and the enthronement of the Antichrist.

> *Zad Rust*
> Teddy Bare *(1972)*

Robert Kennedy (1925–68)

His dealings made Jack Kennedy look like Little Lord Fauntleroy . . . a many-faceted man whose relationships were not limited to the domestic front.

C. David Heymann
Publishers Weekly *(1991)*

A self-important upstart and a know-it-all.

Thomas P. "Tip" O'Neill

Bobby Kennedy is so concerned about poverty because he didn't have any as a kid.

Ronald Reagan (1968)

Henry Kissinger (b 1923)

His compulsion to crow is as natural as a rooster's, to preen as normal as a peacock's.

Robert Hartmann

Kissinger brought peace to Vietnam the same way Napoleon brought peace to Europe: by losing.

Joseph Heller

Henry's idea of sex is to slow down to thirty miles an hour when he drops you off at the door.

Barbara Howar

Satire died the day that Henry Kissinger got the Nobel
Peace Prize.

Tom Lehrer

Ed Koch (b 1924)
Ed Koch is like Richard Nixon. He is forever
rearranging his Enemies List in his mind. Mr.
Koch is a practitioner of political sadomasochism:
inflicting pain gives him pleasure.

Jack Newfield

Fiorello La Guardia (1882–1947)
Anyone who extends to him the right hand of
fellowship is in danger of losing a couple of fingers.

Alva Johnston

G. Gordon Liddy
A knight looking for a liege lord to serve.

Anonymous

John Lindsay
You are nothing but a juvenile, a lightweight, and a
pipsqueak. You have to grow up.

Michael J. Quill

Bruce Lindsey

This colorless, odorless, almost invisible person—who looks like [Prime Minister] John Major in a button-down shirt.

Jeremy Campbell
London Evening Standard
(1992)

Edward Livingstone

He is a man of splendid abilities, but utterly corrupt. Like rotten mackerel by moonlight, he shines and stinks.

John Randolph

Henry Cabot Lodge (1850–1924)

I have long heard of the reputation for wisdom and wit of the senator from Massachusetts, but his speech today has convinced me that his mind is like the land of his native state—barren by nature and impoverished by cultivation.

Thaddeus Caraway (senator)
(1919)

Huey Long (1893–1935)

A Winston Churchill who has never been to Harrow [the elite English boarding school].

H. G. Wells

Norman Mailer (b 1923)

On Mailer's failure to get elected mayor of New York City—All Norman Mailer the politician accomplished was to prove that in New York City almost anyone can get forty-one thousand votes if a million people go to the polls.

Richard Reeves (1969)

Robert Martinez

Governor Martinez exudes the warm personal charm of a millipede.

Dave Barry

Joseph McCarthy (1908–57)

One of the most unlovely characters in our history since Aaron Burr.

Dean Acheson (1954)

He dons his war paint . . . goes into his war dance . . . goes forth to battle and proudly returns with the scalp of a pink Army dentist.

Ralph Flanders

A sadistic bum from Wisconsin.

Hank Greenspun

A pathological character assassin.

Harry S. Truman

Robert McNamara (b 1916)
McNamara voices all the stereotypes of liberal
humanitarianism, but he keeps them free from the
grime of reality. He reminds one of a mid-Victorian
novelist writing without mention of sex or sweat.

I. F. Stone (1968)

Thomas Paine (1737–1809)
Like Judas he will be remembered by posterity; men
will learn to express all that is base, malignant,
treacherous, unnatural, and blasphemous by the single
monosyllable: Paine.

William Cobbett

A mouse nibbling at the wing of an archangel.

Robert Hall

J. Danforth Quayle (b 1947)
After Quayle misspelled "potato"—Dumpe Quayl!

Anonymous banner (1992)

I just know he has the smallest penis. I mean, we're
talking freezing cold acorn in his pants, screaming for
cover.

Carrie Fisher
Esquire

Dan Quayle is more stupid than Ronald Reagan put
together.

Matt Groening (1993)

He represents white bread with no nutritional value whatsoever.

Jarboe (1989)

He's like Robert Redford's retarded brother that they kept up in the attic, and he got out somehow.

Patty Marx

A callow moron.

Philadelphia Daily News

The choice of an utter nincompoop as vice president is absolute insurance against impeachment.

Michael M. Thomas

Nancy Reagan (b 1921)
Nancy Reagan fell down and broke her hair.

Johnny Carson

A senescent bimbo with a lust for home furnishings.

Barbara Ehrenreich

Even her staunchest defenders concede that Nancy Reagan is more Marie Antoinette than Mother Teresa.

Newsweek *(1991)*

Nancy's career is one of . . . social climbing. She was born with a silver ladder in her hand.

Gore Vidal
United States Essays *(1993)*

Thomas B. Reed

He does what he likes, without consulting the administration, which he detests, or his followers, whom he despises.

Cecil Spring-Rice

Walter Reuther

You are like a nightingale. It closes its eyes when it sings and sees nothing and hears nobody but itself.

Nikita Khrushchev

James W. Riley

The unctuous, overcheerful, word-mouthing, flabby-faced citizen who condescendingly tells Providence, in flowery and well-rounded periods, where to get off.

Hewlett Howland

Eugene Talmadge

His chain-gang excellency.

Harold Ickes

Henry Wallace

Henry's the sort of guy that keeps you guessing as to whether he's going to deliver a sermon or wet the bed.

Anonymous

James G. Watt

The Secretary of the Interior has gone bonkers. It's time the white-coat people took him away.

Gaylord Nelson

Daniel Webster (1782–1852)

The most meanly and foolishly treacherous man I ever heard of.

James Russell Lowell

THE PRESIDENCY

Trying to get the presidency to work these days is like trying to sew buttons on a custard pie.

James D. Barber

The office of presidency is such a bastardized thing—half royalty, half democracy—that nobody knows whether to genuflect or spit.

Jimmy Breslin

Remember, everybody, let sleeping dogs lie—but somebody wake up the president.

Bill Cosby
"You Bet Your Life"

Scrubbing floors and emptying bedpans has as much dignity as the presidency.

Richard Nixon

All the president is is a glorified public relations man who spends his time flattering, kissing, and kicking people to get them to do what they are supposed to do anyway.

Harry S. Truman

John Adams (1735–1826)
It has been the political career of this man to begin with hypocrisy, proceed with arrogance, and finish with contempt.

Thomas Paine

John Quincy Adams (1767–1848)
It is said he is a disgusting man to do business with. Coarse and dirty and clownish in his address and stiff and abstracted in his opinions, which are drawn from books exclusively.

William Henry Harrison

Of all the men it was ever my lot to waste civilities
upon, Adams was the most doggedly and systematically
repulsive. With a vinegar aspect, cotton in his leathern
ears . . . he sat in the frivolous assemblies of Petersburg
like a bull-dog among spaniels.

W. H. Lyttleton

Chester A. Arthur (1830–1886)
First in ability on the list of second-rate men.

New York Times *(1872)*

A nonentity with side-whiskers.

Attributed to Woodrow Wilson

James Buchanan (1791–1868)
The Constitution provides for every accidental
contingency in the Executive, except for a vacancy in
the mind of the president.

Senator Sherman of Ohio

Pat Buchanan and Ross Perot
On the minor candidates in the 1994 presidential election—
Two choleric below-the-belt character actors, good for
cutaways when the stars need a rest.

Gore Vidal
New York Times

George Bush (b 1924)

A pin-stripin' polo-playin' umbrella-totin' Ivy Leaguer,
born with a silver spoon so far in his mouth that you
couldn't get it out with a crowbar.

Bill Baxley

He is moaning like a pig stuck under a gate.

Bill Clinton (1992)

George Bush is a fake, a fool, and a wimp.

Jules Feiffer
Village Voice *(1988)*

Replying to Bush's "Bozo" taunt (see page 348)—It must
have been Millie [his dog] that taught him to roll over
and play dead.

Al Gore (1992)

If ignorance ever goes to forty dollars a barrel, I want
drilling rights on George Bush's head.

Jim Hightower (1988)

He's a Boy Scout with a hormone imbalance.

Kevin Phillips

He can't help it—he was born with a silver foot in his
mouth.

Ann Richards

A weaseling pragmatist devoid of principle.

William Safire (1992)

After Bush lost the 1992 presidential campaign—George Bush's mistake was to run a big-band campaign in a rock 'n' roll country.

Ralph Whitehead

George Bush and Dan Quayle
Putting Bush and Quayle in charge of the economy is like making General Sherman the fire marshal of Atlanta.

Bill Clinton (1992)

George Bush, Bill Clinton, and Ross Perot
A wimp, a wonk, and a wacko.

Anonymous (1992)

Jimmy Carter (b 1924)
When Carter gave a fireside chat, the fire went out.

Anonymous

Jimmy Carter has the potential and proclivity of a despot.

Eugene McCarthy (1976)

A hayseed with a toothy grin.

P. J. O'Rourke

Jimmy Carter, Gerald Ford, and Richard Nixon
History buffs probably noted the reunion at a
Washington party a few weeks ago of three ex-
presidents: Carter, Ford, and Nixon—See No Evil,
Hear No Evil, and Evil.

Bob Dole, speech (1983)

Grover Cleveland (1837–1908)
To nominate Grover Cleveland would be to march
through a slaughterhouse into an open grave.

Henry Watterson

Bill Clinton (b 1946)
On Clinton's becoming president—It's a great day for
Arkansas. We're on the map at last. Better still, Bill
Clinton's not our governor anymore.

*Anonymous Arkansas
businesswoman (1992)*

Bill Clinton's foreign policy experience is pretty
much confined to having had breakfast once at the
International House of Pancakes.

Pat Buchanan

A stumblebum, spud-faced Little League lothario.

Julie Burchill (1993)

A two-faced bumpkin from Arkansas.

George Bush (1992)

Being attacked on character by Governor Clinton is like being called ugly by a frog.

George Bush (1992)

Hillary's husband elected.

Die Tageszeitung *(1992)*

Comparing Clinton, his wife, and his running mate to characters from The Wizard of Oz—Al Gore is looking for a brain, Hillary is looking for a heart. I hope the national media is not listening, but people tell me that Clinton is looking for Dorothy.

Bob Dorman (1992)

I'm just sick and tired of presidents who jog. Remember, if Bill Clinton wins, we're going to have another four years of his white thighs flapping in the wind.

Arianna Huffington (1995)

Even I would take offense at being called a liar by a governor of Arkansas, whose career as an evader of truths is hardly less distinguished than Emmett Smith's as an eluder of open-field tackles.

> *Murray Kempton*
> New York Review of Books
> *(1992)*

On Clinton's becoming governor of Arkansas—I hear you have been elected king of some place with two men and a dog.

> *Douglas Millin*

If Bill Clinton is a moderate, then I am a champion speller.

> *Dan Quayle*

Bill Clinton and Bob Dole
Voting for these two is like choosing your favorite Menendez brother.

> *Joan Rivers*
> *"Comedy Central" (1996)*

Bill Clinton and Al Gore
Governor Taxes and Mr. Ozone.

> *George Bush (1992)*

My dog Millie knows more about foreign affairs than these two bozos.

> *George Bush (1992)*

Bill and Hillary Clinton
Compared to the Clintons, Ronald Reagan is living proof that a Republican with half a brain is better than a Democrat with two.

> *P. J. O'Rourke (1997)*

Calvin Coolidge (1872–1933)
Inactivity is a political philosophy and a party program
with Mr. Coolidge.

Walter Lippmann

Dwight D. Eisenhower (1890–1969)
Roosevelt proved that a president could serve for life.
Truman proved that anyone could be a president.
Eisenhower proved that your country can be run
without a president.

Nikita Khrushchev, letter
(1960)

Eisenhower employs the three-monkeys standard of
campaign morality: see no evil—if it's Republican;
hear no evil—unless it's Democratic; and speak no
evil—unless Senator Taft says it's all right.

Adlai Stevenson

Why, this fellow don't know any more about politics
than a pig knows about Sunday.

Harry S. Truman

Eisenhower is the most completely opportunistic and
unprincipled politician America has ever raised to high
office . . . insincere, vindictive, hypocritical, and a
dedicated, conscious agent of the Communist
conspiracy.

Robert H. Weichler

Gerald Ford (b 1913)
He could even f*** up a two-car funeral.

Anonymous

Although he was wrong most of the time, he was
decently wrong.

Thomas P. "Tip" O'Neill

Hark, when Gerald Ford was king
We were bored with everything.
Unemployment six percent,
What a boring president.
Nothing major needed fixin'
So he pardoned Richard Nixon.

*Bill Strauss and Eliana
Newport (1982)*

Warren G. Harding (1865–1923)
His speeches left the impression of an army of
pompous phrases moving over the landscape in search
of an idea.

William McAdoo

His writing is rumble and bumble, flap and doodle,
balder and dash.

H. L. Mencken

A tinhorn politician with the manner of a rural corn doctor and the mien of a ham-doctor.

> *H. L. Mencken*
> Baltimore Evening Sun
> *(1920)*

William Henry Harrison (1773–1841)
An active but shallow mind, a political adventurer not without talents but self-sufficient, vain, and indiscreet.

> *John Quincy Adams*

Herbert Hoover
Hoover is the world's greatest engineer: he's drained, ditched, and damned the United States.

> *Anonymous (1931)*

He wouldn't commit himself to the time of day from a hatful of watches.

> *Westbrook Pegler*

Andrew Jackson (1767–1845)
I cannot believe that the killing of two thousand Englishmen at New Orleans qualifies a person for the various difficult and complicated duties of the presidency.

> *Henry Clay*

Thomas Jefferson (1743–1826)

A mean-spirited, low-livered fellow. There could be no question he would sell his country at the first offer made to him cash down.

Anonymous

A slur upon the moral government of the world.

John Quincy Adams

The moral character of Jefferson was repulsive. Continually puling about liberty, equality, and the degrading curse of slavery, he brought his own children to the hammer, and made money of their debaucheries.

Alexander Hamilton

Lyndon B. Johnson (1908–73)

When Johnson wanted to persuade you of something, you really felt as if a St. Bernard dog had licked your face for an hour.

Ben Bradlee

He turned out to be so many different characters he could have populated all of *War and Peace* and still had a few people left over.

Herbert Mitgang (1980)

People have said that my language was bad, but Jesus! You should have heard LBJ.

Richard Nixon (1976)

Uncle Cornpone and his little Porkchop.

Jacqueline Kennedy Onassis
Newsweek *(1994)*

How does one tell the president of the United States to stop picking his nose, and lifting his leg to fart in front of the TV camera, and using "chickenshit" in every other sentence?

Stuart Rosenberg

John F. Kennedy (1917–63)
A spavined little hunchback.

India Edwards

On Kennedy's death—I hope the worms eat his eyes out.

Jimmy Hoffa (1963)

He'll be remembered for just one thing: he was the first Roman Catholic elected president. Period.

Richard Scammon (1963)

The liberals like his rhetoric and the conservatives like his inaction.

Norman Thomas (1960)

Dick Lamm (b 1935)

On news of life on Mars—Bad news for presidential candidate Dick Lamm. That makes two planets where no one has heard of him.

Jay Leno (1996)

Abraham Lincoln (1809–65)

This man's appearance, his pedigree, his coarse low jokes and anecdotes, his vulgar smiles, and his frivolity are a disgrace to the seat he holds.

John Wilkes Booth

On the Gettysburg address—An offensive exhibition of boorishness and vulgarity.

Chicago Times *(1863)*

His soul seems to be made of leather, and incapable of any grand or noble emotion. Compared with the mass of men, he is a line of flat prose in a beautiful and spirited lyric. He lowers, he never elevates you. . . . Even wisdom from him seems but folly.

New York Post

I say here, in my place in the Senate of the United
States, that I never did see or converse with so weak
and imbecile a man as Abraham Lincoln. . . . If I
wanted to paint a tyrant, if I wanted to paint a despot,
a man perfectly regardless of every constitutional right
of the people, whose sworn servant, not ruler, he is, I
would paint the hideous form of Abraham Lincoln.

Willard Saulsbury (1863)

Richard M. Nixon (1913–95)

Nixon's motto was: If two wrongs don't make a right,
try three.

Norman Cousins

Here is a guy who's had a stake driven through his
heart. I mean, really nailed to the bottom of the coffin
with a wooden stake, and a silver bullet through the
forehead for good measure—and yet he keeps coming
back.

Ted Koppel (1984)

All that stands between the USA and a dictatorship.

L. L. Levinson

He was like a kamikaze pilot who keeps apologizing
for the attack.

Mary McGrory (1962)

He bleeds people. He draws every drop of blood and then drops them from a cliff. He'll blame any person he can put his foot on.

Martha Mitchell (1973)

The Eichmann trial taught the world the banality of evil, now Nixon is teaching the world the evil of banality.

I. F. Stone (1970)

Nixon is a no-good lying bastard. He can lie out of both sides of his mouth at the same time, and even if he caught himself telling the truth, he'd lie just to keep his hand in.

Harry S. Truman

Richard Nixon, Gerald Ford, Jimmy Carter, and Ronald Reagan

A Mount Rushmore of incompetence.

David Steinberg

H. Ross Perot, third-party candidate

A. A. Milne's Piglet come to life.

Bitch *magazine (1993)*

Perot is the sort of man of whom it is said, "In your head, you know he's right; in your guts, you know he's nuts."

Christopher Buckley (1992)

A hand grenade with a bad haircut.

> *Peggy Noonan*
> Forbes *(1992)*

Perot (noun). To Perot: to unexpectedly quit—as in my cellular phone just Perot'd.

> Wired *(1993)*

Franklin Pierce (1804–69)
A small politician, of low capacity and mean surroundings, proud to act as the servile tool of men worse than himself but also stronger and abler. He was ever ready to do any work the slavery leaders set him, and to act as their attorney in arguing in its favor, to quote Benton's phrase, with "undaunted mendacity, moral callosity and mental obliquity."

> *Theodore Roosevelt*
> Life of Thomas Hart Benton
> *(1886)*

Pierce did not know what was going on and even if he had, he wouldn't have known what to do about it.

> *Harry S. Truman*

James Polk (1795–1849)
He seems to be acting on the principle of hanging an old friend for the purpose of making two new ones.

> *Andrew Johnson*

A more ridiculous, contemptible, and forlorn creature was never put forward by any party. Mr. Polk is a sort of fourth- or rather fortieth-rate lawyer and small politician in Tennessee, who by accident was once Speaker of the House.

New York Herald

Ronald Reagan (b 1911)
You could walk through Ronald Reagan's thoughts without getting your feet wet.

Anonymous senator (1980)

Naming a national forest after Ronald Reagan is like naming a day-care center after W. C. Fields.

Bob Hattoy

To listen even briefly to Ronald Reagan is to realize that he is a man upon whose synapses termites have dined long and well.

Christopher Hitchins

The battle for the mind of Ronald Reagan was like trench warfare in World War I: never have so many fought so hard for such barren terrain.

Peggy Noonan

A cheerleader for selfishness.

Thomas P. "Tip" O'Neill

He has achieved a political breakthrough . . . the
Teflon-coated presidency. He sees to it that nothing
sticks to him.

Patricia Schroeder

Franklin D. Roosevelt (1882–1945)
Roosevelt wasn't a bump on a pickle compared to
what I'd have been in the White House.

Huey Long

One-third sap, two-thirds Eleanor.

Alice Roosevelt Longworth

He had every quality that morons esteem in their
heroes. He was the first American to penetrate to the
real depths of vulgar stupidity.

H. L. Mencken

Theodore Roosevelt (1858–1919)
A dangerous and ominous jingoist.

Henry James

The mere monstrous embodiment of unprecedented
resounding noise.

Henry James

Theodore Roosevelt was an old maid with testosterone
poisoning.

Patricia O'Toole

His idea of getting hold of the right end of the stick is to snatch it from the hands of somebody who is using it effectively, and to hit him over the head with it.

George Bernard Shaw

Harold Stassen, perennial third-party candidate
A political nymphomaniac.

Relman Morin

Adlai Stevenson
On Stevenson's running for office again—It was like a man marrying his mistress, long after the flames of passion have flickered and gone out, because he is used to her and needs someone to darn his socks.

Joseph W. Alsop (1956)

Zachary Taylor (1784–1850)
Quite ignorant for his rank, and quite bigoted in his ignorance. Few men have ever had a more comfortable, labor-saving contempt for learning of every kind.

Winfield Scott
Memoirs *(1864)*

10
FOREIGN BODIES

Idi Amin, Ugandan dictator (b 1925)

Amin? He's just a goddamn cannibal! A goddamn
asshole. He'd eat his own mother. Christ . . . he'd eat
his own grandmother!

Richard Nixon

Harold C. Banks, Canadian union leader

He is the stuff of the Capones and the Hoffas, of
whom the dictators throughout history, from the
earliest times to the totalitarians, Hitler and Stalin, are
prototypes. He is a bully, cruel, dishonest, greedy,
power-hungry, contemptuous of the law.

Canadian Royal
Commission *(1963)*

Tony Blair, British prime minister
A second-rate nobody with bouffant hair and a silly smile.

Private Eye (1994)

Pieter W. Botha, South African president
His head is so deeply buried in the sand that you will have to recognize him by the shape of his toes.

Gatsha Buthelezi (1987)

British Royal Family (House of Windsor)
They were never the family next door. They are a very strange Gothic, German dynasty. It took Diana to tell just how very weird that family is. They're like "The Munsters" or something.

Julie Burchill (1997)

The Royal Family . . . you can't live with them, and the Irish can't seem to blow them up.

Bill Maher
"Politically Incorrect" (1993)

Julius Caesar, Roman emperor (100–44 B.C.)
A man of great common sense and good taste—meaning thereby a man without originality or moral courage.

George Bernard Shaw

(Sir) Winston Churchill,
British prime minister (1874–1965)

He has spoilt himself by reading about Napoleon.

David Lloyd George

Moshe Dayan, Israeli foreign minister (1915–81)

Don't be so humble, you're not that great.

Golda Meir

Charles de Gaulle, French president (1890–1970)

He looks like a female llama surprised in her bath.

Winston Churchill

General de Gaulle is again pictured in our newspapers looking as usual like an embattled codfish. I wish he could be filleted and put quietly away in a refrigerator.

Sylvia Townsend Warner

Jacques Delors, European Community president

He is like a Turkish carpet salesman, applying rudeness, finesse, insight, and diplomatic skill, while promising more than he really has.

Anonymous member of the
E.C. Council of Ministers

He is like a slimy dead sheep stuffed down the back of a sofa.

Private Eye

John G. Diefenbaker, Canadian prime minister
(1895–1979)

The besetting disease of Canadian public life for
almost a decade had been Diefenbakerism: the belief
that promises were policies, that rhetoric was action,
and that the electorate believe in Santa Claus.

> *Ramsay Cook*
> The Maple Leaf Forever
> *(1971)*

It is scarcely an exaggeration to say that fewer tears
were shed over the fall of Canadian Prime Minister
John Diefenbaker than over the upset of any major
Commonwealth political figure since Oliver
Cromwell.

> *Robert Estabrook*
> Washington Post *(1963)*

A platitudinous bore.

> *John F. Kennedy*

King Edward VIII of England (1894–1972)

The most damning epitaph you can compose about
Edward is one that all comfortable people should
cower from deserving: he was at his best only when
the going was good.

> *Alistair Cooke*
> Six Men

He had hidden shallows.

> *Clive James*

King Edward VIII and Wallis Simpson

Reviewing Philip Ziegler's biography Edward VIII
(1990)—This book confirms Edward VIII as the
nastiest human being in twentieth-century British
history . . . with the possible exception of his wife
[Wallis Simpson].

> *Paul Foot*
> London Correspondent

Albert Einstein, German-born physicist

(1879–1955)
I'd have given ten conversations with Einstein for a
first meeting with a pretty chorus girl.

> *Albert Camus*

As a rational scientist, Einstein is a fair violinist.
Einstein is already dead and buried alongside
Andersen, Grimm, and the Mad Hatter.

> *George F. Gilette (1929)*

The genius of Einstein leads to Hiroshima.

> *Pablo Picasso (1946)*

Queen Elizabeth I of England (1533–1603)

As just and merciful as Nero, and as good a Christian
as Mahomet.

> *John Wesley*
> Journal *(1768)*

Queen Elizabeth II of England (b 1926)
Her annual Christmas broadcast to the Commonwealth
is a dull highlight of any year, which only watching
The Great Escape for the twelfth time afterwards can
match.

> *Peter Freedman*
> Glad to Be Gray *(1985)*

A piece of cardboard that they drag round on a trolley.

> *John Lydon (1977)*

Sarah Ferguson, Duchess of York (b 1959)
The Duchess of Pork.

> *British tabloid newspaper*
> *nickname*

Britain's favorite slag.

> *Louise Doughty*

She is very greedy when it comes to loot, and wants
to upstage everybody.

> *Nicholas Fairbairn*

Francisco Franco, Spanish dictator (1892–1975)
A small, rather corpulent bourgeoisie, with the voice
of a doctor with a good bedside manner.

> *Sir Samuel Hoare (1937)*

Malcolm Fraser, Australian prime minister
(b 1930)

He is the cutlery man of Australia. He was born with a silver spoon in his mouth, speaks with a forked tongue, and knifes his colleagues in the back.

Bob Hawke (1975)

Sigmund Freud, Austrian psychoanalyst
(1856–1939)

I always loathed the Viennese quack. I used to stalk him down dark alleys of thought, and now we shall never forget the sight of old, flustered Freud, seeking to unlock his door with the point of his umbrella.

Vladimir Nabokov

Mohandas "Mahatma" Gandhi,
Indian political leader (1869–1948)

Gandhi has been assassinated. In my humble opinion a bloody good thing but far too late.

Noël Coward
Diary *(1948)*

King George V of England (1865–1936)
Lousy but loyal.

Anonymous jubilee banner
(1935)

If he ever sets foot in Chicago, I'll punch him in the snoot.

William H. Thompson

Che Guevara, Bolivian-born revolutionary
(1928–67)
Guevara was a powerful theoretician but no soldier.

Shelford Bidwell
Modern Warfare *(1973)*

King Hassan of Morocco and the Shah of Iran
Both of them, playboys at one time, are so serious now
that they are kings. They must be overcompensating.

John F. Kennedy

Charles Haughey, Irish prime minister (b 1925)
I have a theory about Charles Haughey. Give him
enough rope and he'll hang you.

Leo Enright (1992)

If I saw Mr. Haughey buried at midnight at a
crossroads, with a stake driven through his heart—
politically speaking—I should continue to wear a clove
of garlic round my neck, just in case.

Conor Cruise O'Brien

Adolf Hitler, German dictator (1889–1945)
Hitler has the advantage of a man who knows the
theater only from the gallery.

Bertolt Brecht (1923)

Hitler's achievements as Supreme Commander in the Second World War were inferior to his achievements as an ordinary soldier in the First.

> *J. Strawson*
> Hitler as a Military Leader
> *(1971)*

He is formless, almost faceless, a man whose countenance is a caricature, a man whose framework seems cartilaginous without bones. He is inconsequent and voluble, ill-poised, insecure. He is the very prototype of the Little Man.

> *Dorothy Thompson*

King Hussein of Jordan (1935–99)
During the Israeli–PLO peace talks—Hussein isn't just sitting on the fence . . . he is the fence.

> *Anonymous American diplomat*
> *(1995)*

On Queen Noor's visit to London after the Persian Gulf War—I think she's come to London to get a pair of pliers to get the splinters out of her husband's backside. He's sat on the fence so long, I think the little wretch should stay out of this country and keep his family with him.

> *Terry Dicks*

Dolores Ibarruri (La Pasionaria), Spanish revolutionary (1895–1989)
One of the most despicable and self-seeking careerists of the Communist movement.

Franz Borkenau

Joseph Joffre, French field marshal (1852–1931)
The only time he put up a fight in his life was when we asked him for his resignation.

Georges Clemenceau

Carl Jung, Swiss psychiatrist (1875–1961)
Jung's latter-day philosophy, with its esoteric archtripe, fitted wonderfully with the Nazi endeavor to befuddle people's minds, make them mistrust the evidence of their own senses, and obey an elite with pure blood and impure motives.

Frederic Wertham

Radovan Karadzic, Serbian president (b 1945)
A rambling, inconsistent, sentimental, bouffanted crook.

John Naughton (1992)

Paul Keating, Australian prime minister (b 1954)
Appearance: Chevy Chase crossed with an albino raisin.

London Guardian *(1993)*

Muammar Khaddhafi, Libyan dictator (b 1942)
You don't go out and kick a mad dog. If you have a
mad dog with rabies, you take a gun and shoot it.

Pat Robertson

**Ruhollah Khomeini, Iranian ayatollah
(religious leader)** (1901–89)
A lunatic.

*Anwar Sadat
(president of Egypt)*

(Sir) Wilfrid Laurier, Canadian prime minister
(1841–1919)
He was never any good at figures, other than those of
speech.

Paul Bilkey (1940)

Vladimir I. Lenin, Russian premier (1870–1924)
It was with a sense of awe that the Germans turned
upon Russia the most grisly of all weapons. They
transported Lenin in a sealed truck like a plague
bacillus from Switzerland into Russia.

Winston Churchill
The World Crisis *(1929)*

You show the bourgeoisie your behind. We, on the
contrary, look them in the face.

Georgi Piekhanov (1895)

King Louis XIV of France (1638–1715)
Strip your Louis Quatourze of his king-gear, and there
is left nothing but a poor forked radish with a head
fantastically carved.

Thomas Carlyle

John Major, British prime minister (b 1943)
Why does it take two days for a Polaroid of John
Major to appear?

Barry Cryer (1992)

He is such a nonentity that if his life flashed before his
eyes, he wouldn't be in it.

David Lange (1994)

He makes George Bush seem like a personality.

Jackie Mason

Richard Nixon played as farce, with a script by
Machiavelli.

Andrew Rawnsley (1994)

**Nelson Mandela and F. W. De Klerk,
South African presidents**
On their sharing the 1994 Nobel Peace Prize—The
Closest of Strangers.

Washington Post *headline*

Imelda Marcos, wife of Philippines President Ferdinand Marcos

She is a kind of cross between the middle-aged Merle Oberon and the juvenile Elvis Presley.

Bob Colacello

Arthur Meighen, Canadian prime minister
(1874–1960)
Meighen had the gift of being admired by those who agreed with him.

C. G. Power (1966)

Benito Mussolini, Italian dictator (1883–1945)
Mussolini is the biggest bluff in Europe.

Ernest Hemingway
Toronto Daily Star *(1923)*

A promoted clown.

A. J. P. Taylor

Napoleon Bonaparte, emperor of France
(1769–1821)
If utter selfishness, if the reckless sacrifice of humanity to your own interest and passions be vileness, history has no viler name.

Goldwin Scott
Three English Statesmen
(1807)

Napoleon III of France
His mind was a kind of extinct sulfur-pit.

Thomas Carlyle

(Sir) Isaac Newton, English scientist (1642–1727)
I believe the souls of five hundred Sir Isaac Newtons
would go to the making up of a Shakespeare or
Milton.

*Samuel Taylor Coleridge, letter
(1801)*

Manuel Noriega, Panamanian general
He is a bad guy in a pulp crime novel . . . a
narcoterrorist.

George Bush (1989)

George Papandreou, Greek prime minister
A garrulous, senile windbag without power of decision
or resolution.

Dean Acheson (1964)

Louis Pasteur, French chemist (1822–95)
It is absurd to think that germs causing fermentation
and putrefaction come from the air; the atmosphere
would have to be as thick as pea soup for that.

Dr. Nicolas Joly

Pol Pot, Cambodian dictator

He makes Idi Amin look like the Dalai Lama.

David Wallis
Esquire *(1997)*

Bertrand Russell, Welsh philosopher (1872–1970)

One of the most fabulously stupid men of our age.

Brian Appleyard

Poor Bertrand Russell, he's all Disembodied Mind.

D. H. Lawrence

U Thant, Burmese United Nations secretary-general (1909–74)

Will somebody please get rid of that little yellow bastard?

Lyndon B. Johnson

Margaret Thatcher, British prime minister (b 1925)

Mrs. Thatcher may be a woman, but she isn't a sister.

Anonymous feminist (1979)

The great She-elephant, who must be obeyed. . . . She is the Castro of the Western world—an embarrassment to her friends—all she lacks is a beard.

Denis Healey (1990)

The new one-pound coin should be called the
"Thatcher," because it's thick, brassy, and wanted
to be a sovereign.

David Prowse

Leon Trotsky, Russian commissar (1879–1940)
He possessed in his nature all the qualities requisite for
the art of civil destruction: the organizing command
of a Carnot, the cold detached intelligence of a
Machiavelli, the mob oratory of a Cleon, the ferocity
of Jack the Ripper, the toughness of a Titus Oates.

Winston Churchill
Great Contemporaries *(1937)*

Margaret Trudeau, wife of Pierre Trudeau
(b 1949)
The United States has its first lady; Canada has its
worst lady.

Craig Russell (1979)

Pierre Trudeau, Canadian prime minister (b 1919)
Canada has at last produced a political leader worthy of
assassination.

Irving Layton

Queen Victoria of England (1819–1901)
A mixture of national landlady and actress.

V. S. Pritchett

Kurt Waldheim, United Nations secretary-general
(b 1918)
The only man who could bend over backwards and forwards at the same time.

The Times of London (1985)

Lech Walesa, Polish president (b 1947)
He was an extraordinary leader of workers. He is a terrible head of state.

Gustav Herling (1992)

Charles Windsor, Prince of Wales (b 1948)
Prince Charles loves nostalgia—pitched roofs, pastiche, detail, Victorian architecture. The institution of monarchy is preposterous in a technological society— you can't wear a crown in midtown Manhattan. But if the gentry are in the Palladian houses, the stoical artisans in the pebble-dash house tugging their forelocks—if you re-create the past, then the institution of monarchy and class privilege is tenable.

J. G. Ballard

On the birth of their first son, William—Thank goodness he hasn't got ears like his father.

Princess Diana (1982)

All the speeches on the rainforests and the buildings pale when you're two-timing the most popular woman in England.

Anthony Holden (1992)

Charles and Diana Windsor

Prince Charles is an insensitive, hypocritical oaf and
Princess Diana is a selfish, empty-headed bimbo. They
should never have got married in the first place. I
blame the parents.

Richard Littlejohn
London Sun

Diana Windsor, Princess of Wales (1961–97)

Diana:

1. Roman goddess of hunting.
2. British goddess of shopping and film premieres.

Mike Barfield
The Oldie *(1992)*

Saint Diana the Good. Another day, another theme
park. The patron saint of mothers schleps her children
backward and forward in her endless PR war with
Prince Charles.

Cosmopolitan *(1994)*

Boris Yeltsin, Russian premier (b 1931)

His bypass operation was very successful. Doctors say
he'll soon be able to start binge drinking again.

Jim Mullen
Entertainment Weekly *(1996)*

INDEX